MASTERS

of

WISDOM

JEREMY P. TARCHER/PENGUIN
an imprint of Penguin Random House
New York

MASTERS

of

WISDOM

THE MAHATMAS, THEIR LETTERS, AND THE PATH

EDWARD ABDILL

JEREMY P. TARCHER/PENGUIN
An imprint of Penguin Random House LLC
375 Hudson Street
New York, New York 10014

Most Tarcher/Penguin books are available at special quantity discounts for bulk
purchase for sales promotions, premiums, fund-raising, and educational needs.
Special books or book excerpts also can be created to fit specific needs.
For details, write: SpecialMarkets@penguinrandomhouse.com.

Library of Congress Cataloging-in-Publication Data

Abdill, Edward.
Master of wisdom : the mahatmas, their letters, and the path / Edward Abdill.
p.   cm.
Includes bibliographical references and index.
ISBN 978-0-399-17107-9
1. Theosophy—History.   2. Blavatsky, H.P. (Helena Petrovna), 1831–1891.   1. Title.
BP530.A23   2015   2015000005
299'.93409—dc23

Printed in the United States of America
1   3   5   7   9   10   8   6   4   2

Book design by Meighan Cavanaugh

To Our Elder Brothers

In profound gratitude for all they have done for humanity

ACKNOWLEDGMENTS

It should be obvious that a book such as this could never come to light without the valuable advice and help of a select few. Following are those who have my thanks for making a major contribution to this work.

Dr. John Algeo, Distinguished Professor of English emeritus from the University of Georgia, did an initial edit of the manuscript with such skill that only a few minor changes were necessary. John is past president of the Theosophical Society in America, past international vice president of the Theosophical Society (Adyar, India), and a friend for many years. His assistance has been invaluable.

Joy Mills, an international speaker for the Theosophical Society, past president of the Theosophical Society in America, and a past vice president of the International Society (Adyar), pointed out that Madame Blavatsky may have had a private meeting with Morya in the Shell Grotto in Margate, rather than in Hyde Park. I frequently draw upon her encyclopedic knowledge of Theosophy.

Michael Gomes, a Theosophical historian and author of several books and articles on Theosophical history, has willingly supplied me with whatever information I needed for this book and for my previous book, *The Secret Gateway*.

Dr. Brian Harding, a physicist from Brisbane, Australia, and a Theosophist, provided invaluable assistance on the science chapter of this book.

My wife of forty years, Mary, whose computer expertise saved me from more than one disaster, has provided loving support and encouragement. Her suggestions have frequently helped me to better phrase concepts, and on occasion to add a point to the book that I would otherwise have missed.

Janet Kerschner, the archivist at the Theosophical Society in America, sent me printable copies of one of the original Mahatma Letters, the spirit picture of Stainton Moses, and the portraits of Masters Koot Hoomi and Morya that are included in the book.

Mitch Horowitz, editor in chief and vice president of Tarcher/Penguin, asked me to write this book.

The debt I owe to two Theosophical luminaries, Fritz Kunz, from whom I learned Theosophical metaphysics, and Dora Kunz, his wife, from whom I learned how to meditate, can only be repaid by doing whatever I can to bring the light of Theosophy to others.

Finally, thanks to all others who have assisted in any way that they could. These include but are not limited to Pablo Sender, Nicholas Weeks, Terry Hunt, and Denise O'Keefe.

CONTENTS

PART II

THE PATH

INTRODUCTION

Who can say when it all began? The details are sketchy at best. If we are to believe Helena Petrovna Blavatsky, or H.P.B. as she was known to her friends, it began for her when, as a child, she had psychic visions of a tall Indian man she believed to be her protector. About 1845, when H.P.B. was thirteen, she was nearly killed when a horse she was riding "became frightened and bolted—with her foot caught in the stirrup. She felt someone's arms around her body supporting her until the horse was stopped" (CW l:xxxiii). She thought her protector had saved her. That is hardly convincing evidence for most, and certainly not convincing for anyone who believes there is no such thing as psychic ability. Yet, as Shakespeare wrote: "There are more things in heaven and earth, Horatio, / Than are dreamt of in your philosophy" (*Hamlet*, Act I, Sc. 5, lines 167–168).

Over time, we all develop a worldview, and we most certainly do not all see the world in the same way. Rare are individuals whose minds are open to possibilities beyond what they believe to be true at any given time. Some set their views so firmly in proverbial stone that facts will never confuse them. In the mid-twentieth century, a college psychology major by the name of John Kunz reported that he assisted in a psychological experiment concerning what has been called "ESP" (extrasensory perception). Thousands of questionnaires concerning ESP were sent to psychologists all across the United States. One of the questions asked was, "Do you believe there is such a thing as ESP?" As was to be expected, many answered yes and many more answered no. There was one response, however, that stunned John Kunz and the professor in charge of the experiment. The respondent wrote, "No. I don't believe there is any such thing as ESP. There is no evidence to support the claim, and if there were, I wouldn't believe it." Unfortunately, that response is more common than we might wish. An inquiring mind is neither gullible nor incredulous. Evidence and eyewitness accounts of phenomena and encounters with Masters presented in this book will undoubtedly challenge the worldview of many. A consideration of Blavatsky's claims will begin that challenge.

Blavatsky claimed that, as a young adult, she met in the flesh the man of her childhood psychic visions and learned that he went by the name of "Morya." Later she also met Morya's close colleague, Koot Hoomi, and several other extraordinary men known as "Mahatmas," "Adepts," "Masters" (in the sense of teachers), or simply "the Brothers." She reported that they had extraordinary powers, but that those powers were latent in everyone and, over many lifetimes, would be developed by all. In 1888, in an article in her magazine, *Lucifer*, Blavatsky explained that the names "Morya" and "Koot Hoomi" are pseudonyms because none of the Masters ever give out their real names to the public.[1]

If we had we only the word of Blavatsky, we would have only hearsay evidence for the existence of these amazing men. Not only would hearsay evidence be unacceptable in a court of law, but it would not be sufficient evidence for any reasonable person, even an open-minded one. Fortunately, we do have some hard evidence that these men existed. We have letters written by them.

From their letters and from reports from Blavatsky and others, it is clear that the Masters wanted an organization formed that would spread their knowledge around the world. The central purpose of that organization was to form a nucleus of the universal brotherhood of humanity. In one of his letters, Koot Hoomi, who usually signed his name with the initials "K.H.," wrote, "The *Chiefs* want a 'Brotherhood of Humanity,' a real Universal Fraternity started; an institution which would make itself known throughout the world and arrest the attention of the highest minds" (ML, letter 12, p. 39). That "Fraternity" became the Theosophical Society, whose principal founders were H. P. Blavatsky, Henry Steel Olcott, and William Quan Judge.

---

1. Blavatsky used *Lucifer* in its original Latin sense of "The Light Bearer." She did it partly because she wanted to show that Lucifer was not Satan. She also wanted to get back at the missionaries who were persecuting her. Unfortunately, it all backfired. It simply gave the enemies of Theosophy a chance to say that Theosophy was a satanic cult.

The organization was officially launched in New York on November 17, 1875, with Olcott as its first president, Blavatsky as its corresponding secretary, and Judge as its legal counsel.

In his inaugural address, Olcott announced that the "declared objects" of the Society were "To collect and diffuse a knowledge of the laws which govern the universe." Over the years these objectives were modified, but the goal of those original objectives was never fundamentally changed. The founders were convinced that if the laws governing the universe were understood, it would become clear that the universe, including humanity, arises out of a fundamental unity of substance and consciousness. Hence, universal brotherhood would be revealed as a fact in nature rather than simply as an ideal to be realized. Today, the first object of the Society emphasizes brotherhood, and the second and third objects suggest ways of realizing that brotherhood. The objectives of the Society today are:

- To form a nucleus of the universal brotherhood of humanity, without distinction of race, creed, sex, caste, or color.
- To encourage the comparative study of religion, philosophy, and science.
- To investigate unexplained laws of nature and the powers latent in humanity.

In a letter to Alfred Percy Sinnett, K.H. gives an abridged version of the view of his own superior, the Maha Chohan, on the Theosophical Society. In it there is a curious statement about the objectives of the Society. The Chohan points out that "the main objects of the T.S. are misinterpreted by those who are most willing to serve us" (LMW1:6). The objectives as stated seem easy enough to understand, so what might the Chohan have meant? The misunderstanding may have been due to what is meant by "a nucleus of the universal brotherhood of humanity."

One of the objectives of 1889 read: "To keep alive in man his spiritual intuitions." Intuition, in the Theosophical sense, means insight, and insight comes from *buddhi,* an aspect of the inner self of every human being. When we are functioning in the state of consciousness called "buddhi," we perceive unity. We perceive the whole, which is greater than the sum of its parts. That state of consciousness transcends the personal: it is a state of consciousness in which we perceive humanity as a whole. It is a state wherein the individual senses a unity with all and yet does not lose individuality. By effort, meditation, and an altruistic way of life, we can become one with that inner self from which all insights derive. In deep meditation, we can get a sense of humanity as a whole. When we do, we become aware of the influence streaming from our own inner connections to the One Self, rooted in buddhi. Those who get that sense and identify with it are forming a nucleus of the universal brotherhood of humanity. Individuals even unknown to one another are forming a bond at the deepest level of their being. That bond of unity is a nucleus of the universal brotherhood of humanity.

Those who sense that the consciousness in them is identical with the consciousness in all others are forming that nucleus. Those who sense the divine life in themselves, and sense that same divine life in others, are forming that nucleus. Those who identify with the inner self are forming that nucleus. Those who sense that the Self is one are forming that nucleus. When we sense those inner realities, buddhi itself is being strengthened as its influence extends more and more into our brain consciousness and life. When that happens in the consciousness of even one person, it becomes a powerful influence on others who have not yet sensed it.

The Theosophical Society was meant to be an organization in which members from every culture would unite and work together to help all people realize their underlying unity with humanity as a whole and to experience that unity as the divine spark of life in all of us. We often identify ourselves as Christians, Jews, Hindus, Americans, Asians, Africans, Russians, atheists, and even Theosophists. Yet none of those labels describes who we really are. In fact, we are just basically human beings. The labels do no more than describe our beliefs, cultures, conditioning, places of birth, preferences for one religion or another—or for none. Many recognize the truth of that concept, but few feel with every fiber of their being that they are, at root, one with humanity as a whole.

Even those among us who respect all cultures may not sense the divine spark of life in every person they meet. We are likely to judge others by their appearances. We see only a Polaroid snapshot of those we meet, and we tend to judge them by the tiny bit of information that the photo provides. We human beings are extraordinarily complex. One moment we may appear as saints and in the next moment as devils. It is easy to feel unity with someone who is displaying their saintly side, but not so easy to feel it when they are showing their diabolical side.

The Theosophical Society has no required beliefs. No matter what a person believes, anyone in sympathy with its three objectives is welcome to join the Society. Members are not required to believe even in the existence of the Masters. It must be pointed out, however, that there is a huge difference between being a member of the Society and being a true Theosophist. The number of members is always greater than the number of true Theosophists, and many who have never heard of the Society are Theosophists in spirit. Blavatsky pointed out that

> Any person of average intellectual capacities, and a leaning toward the meta-physical; of pure, unselfish life, who finds more joy in helping his neighbour than in receiving help himself; one who is ever ready to sacrifice his own pleasures for the sake of other people; and who loves Truth, Goodness and Wisdom for their own sake, not for the benefit they may confer—is a Theosophist. (CW 9:155)

According to the Masters and H.P.B., that kind of life leads to wisdom and eventually to adeptship.

In 1879, H.P.B. and Olcott moved the headquarters of the Society from New York to Bombay (now Mumbai), India. At that time, A. P. Sinnett, a well-educated and prominent Englishman living in India, was editor of *The Pioneer*, a leading English-language newspaper published in Allahabad. Sinnett was intrigued by Theosophical philosophy and the phenomena reportedly produced by Blavatsky, so he wrote to Olcott to invite him and Blavatsky to visit him and his wife. In December 1879, Olcott and Blavatsky accepted the invitation and spent some time with the Sinnetts in Allahabad. During that visit, the Sinnetts joined the Theosophical Society.

Like many other well-placed Englishmen in India at that time, the Sinnetts had a summer home in Simla (a city north of Delhi and the summer capital of India at the time of the Raj). In 1880, the founders paid a second visit to the Sinnetts at their summer home there. It was in Simla that H.P.B. performed some amazing phenomena that she attributed to the Masters. Sinnett was duly impressed and accepted the phenomena as valid. Later he wrote a book, *The Occult World*, in which he emphasized the authenticity of the phenomena H.P.B. performed.

Sinnett was a practical man with a scientific mind. He wanted to know more about the laws that governed the amazing phenomena he had witnessed, and he wanted to know more about the Masters who, according to H.P.B., had produced the phenomena. In fact, it was not the Masters who produced most of the phenomena, but H.P.B. herself. In her zeal and admiration for her Teachers, she attributed the most amazing phenomena to them. K.H. told Sinnett that, by attributing the phenomena to the Masters, H.P.B. thought she was adding to their glory, but K.H. said:

> by attributing to us very often phenomena of the most childish nature, she but lowered us in the public estimation and sanctioned the claim of her enemies that she was "but a me-

dium"! But it was of no use. In accordance with our rules, M. was not permitted to forbid her such a course. . . . She had to be allowed full and entire freedom of action, the liberty of *creating causes* that became in due course of time her scourge, her public pillory. He could at best forbid her producing phenomena, and to this last extremity he resorted as often as he could, to her friends' and theosophists' great dissatisfaction. . . . The stereotyped phrase: "It is *not* I; I can do nothing by myself . . . it is all they—the Brothers . . . I am but their humble and devoted slave and instrument" is a downright *fib*. She can and did produce phenomena, owing to her natural powers combined with several long years of regular training, and her phenomena are sometimes better, more wonderful and far more perfect than those of some high, initiated chelas [students], whom she surpasses in artistic taste and purely Western appreciation of art. (ML, letter 92, pp. 295–296)

Having witnessed the amazing phenomena that he believed the Brothers had produced and being desirous of getting in touch with those Brothers and learning about the laws that enabled such phenomena to be produced, Sinnett asked Blavatsky if she thought they would respond to him if he wrote them a letter. She doubted that any of them would consent to that, but she promised Sinnett she would try, and she did.

First, she went to her own teacher, the Mahatma Morya, often known as the Master M. He flat out refused, even though later he did engage in some correspondence with Sinnett. Blavatsky tried several other adepts and finally got one to say he would take up the challenge. That was the Mahatma Koot Hoomi, known usually as K.H. Although the names of Morya and Koot Hoomi are anonyms, they used those names in their letters and have been known by them ever since.

Sinnett wrote his first letter "To the Unknown Brother" and gave it to H.P.B. to deliver. He was so anxious to get answers to his questions that he wrote a second letter before getting a reply to his first. He did finally get a reply, however, and the correspondence between him and K.H. went on for several years. Sinnett kept all the letters from K.H. and Morya, and after Sinnett's death the letters were edited in 1921 by the English Theosophist A. Trevor Barker. They were published in 1923 as *The Mahatma Letters to A. P. Sinnett*. Since that date there have been several editions of the letters, the most recent being the *Mahatma Letters to A. P. Sinnett from the Mahatmas M. and K.H. in Chronological Sequence*, edited by Vicente Hao Chin, Jr. Earlier editions of the letters attempted to group them by subject matter. That was a noble attempt to gather together letters on a given topic, but it presented a serious problem. Individual letters cover more than one topic. So a large part of one letter may deal with the spiritual life, but it may also include comments about science or philosophy.

Because we do not have the original letters that Sinnett sent to the Brothers, we must rely solely on the letters that Sinnett received. From those letters we can only infer what questions Sinnett asked and what comments he may have made. It is much like hearing one side of a telephone conversation. Also, the letters contain much that was pertinent at the time but that is irrelevant now. The adept may have been warning Sinnett about someone whose motives were impure and who might have harmed the Theosophical movement. That was important then but not now. Some letters are primarily about individuals who were either useful or harmful to the movement. Yet in the same letter we may find a line of priceless advice for us today.

The advantage of the chronological edition of the letters is twofold. First, it avoids the inevitable confusion that comes from reading things out of sequence. Second, the chronological edition provides a wealth of historical information for most of the letters. It helps the reader to understand what was going on at the time the letter was written, and it gives some background information on the people mentioned in the letters. The letters themselves are basically the same in all editions, so one need not be concerned that one edition or another is missing any of them.

The original letters were donated to the British Museum in London, but are now housed in the British Library there. The museum accepted the letters for three basic reasons: First of all, they were of historical interest. The British ruled India at the time, and the Theosophical Society was big news in India of the 1880s. Before the Mahatma Letters were published, Annie Besant, a British citizen of Irish descent, became the second international president of the Society. She worked with Mohandas Gandhi to get home rule for India, and while she did not always agree with Gandhi, she became the first president of the home-rule Congress Party. Second, handwriting experts from the museum determined that whoever wrote the Mahatma Letters, they were not written by Blavatsky. Third, many of the letters that were allegedly "precipitated," that is, delivered by phenomenal means rather than by post, have a curious look to them. It appears as though the ink is embedded in the paper, as though the writing and the paper were produced at the same time, and each individual word of every letter looks as though it had been produced by a dot matrix printer, except that instead of dots, each letter consists of tiny dashes. The museum authorities had no explanation for these strange facts. The original letters can be seen in the British Library, where these curious conditions can be personally observed. An enlarged fragment from Mahatma letter 86 showing the peculiar dashes is reproduced here.

There is also a DVD on the Mahatma Letters available from the Theosophical Society in America that shows photographs of the original letters, including those that were phenomenally produced.

There will always be those who say the whole idea of Masters was fabricated by Blavatsky. Yet, as any detective knows, one must look for motive as well as means and opportunity. H.P.B. may have had the means and the opportunity, but what could possibly have been her motive? She got no money for passing the letters on; she was called a fraud and liar; she was betrayed more than once; and her personal fame was more one of infamy than praise. In addition to all that, the letters seem to have one main purpose, that of helping humanity. The Masters often stressed the need for a universal brotherhood. They asked for and received nothing for themselves. On the contrary, they had to put up with slander and verbal attacks from many who thought themselves vastly superior to dark-skinned Indians.

By allowing the Masters to speak for themselves through their letters, they may become living men to the reader. In this book, you will also find much of what they taught through the words of their direct agent, H. P. Blavatsky. By no means was everything written by her authorized by the Masters, but what is quoted from her is almost certainly what she learned from them. Only a small portion of what the Masters taught is presented in this book, and that, according to them, is but a fragment of what they know to be true about our universe and us who inhabit it. I hope that those who read this book will give Blavatsky and the Mahatmas a fair hearing and read what they had to say with an open and unprejudiced mind.

PART I

THE MAHATMAS AND
THEIR LETTERS

Chapter 1

BLAVATSKY AND THE MAHATMAS

Blavatsky claims that she first met Morya in London in 1851 at the time of the Great Exhibition, which was what we would call a "world fair." She was observing a parade of delegates from the British colonies and suddenly recognized her "protector" in the Nepal delegation. She rushed out to greet him, but he waved her back. She told Countess Constance Wachtmeister that the next day she met Morya in Hyde Park. While she may have met him there, it is possible that Morya asked her to meet him elsewhere for a private talk. Hyde Park had been covered over by a glass dome called the Crystal Palace, and the entire park was filled with visitors from all over the world. There would have been little space for privacy. Evidence for a private meeting elsewhere comes from a diary found in an old trunk that Blavatsky's Aunt Nadyezhda sent to the countess shortly after H.P.B. had told the countess of her encounter with Morya. The countess reports that in a diary entry written in French on

August 12, 1851, Blavatsky wrote, "Memorable night . . . when I met the Master of my dreams" in Ramsgate. She added that the meeting occurred on her twentieth birthday, July 31 by the Russian calendar. The countess asked Blavatsky why she had written "Ramsgate" rather than "London," and H.P.B. responded that Ramsgate was "a blind." It is strange that she would have said she met Morya in London and then said it was in Ramsgate, stranger still that she claimed Ramsgate was a blind. The riddle may be solved if we consider the possibility that Ramsgate was a blind for Margate, which is adjacent to Ramsgate. In Margate there is a grotto called "the Shell Grotto." It has walls covered with shells depicting suns, flowers, trees, animals, and something that appears to be an altar. The grotto was discovered by accident in 1835, and to this day no one knows who covered the walls with shell designs or why. It would have been an extremely private place to meet, and one might conjecture that the atmosphere was spiritually charged and undisturbed from the day the cave was made into a temple. Perhaps Blavatsky used the blind of Ramsgate because she did not want the atmosphere in the Shell Grotto in Margate to be polluted by curiosity seekers.

No matter where Morya and Blavatsky met, their conversation was almost certainly about a mission the Masters wanted H.P.B. to carry out. Morya told H.P.B. that for years he and his colleagues had been looking for someone who might help Westerners learn something of their philosophy and their understanding of our universe and the human condition, especially the spiritual nature of humanity. He told her that she was far from perfect, but she was the best available spokesperson for them at the time. While they did not say why she was the best, it is not unreasonable to suppose that there were several reasons she was chosen.

Without doubt, H.P.B. was one of the greatest psychics of modern times. Her paranormal ability has been attested to by many reliable witnesses, from her relatives in Russia when she was a child, to friends, associates, and acquaintances throughout her life. For the Masters to communicate easily with anyone requires what might be called a "clear psychic link." Master M. or K.H. could send a thought telepathically to H.P.B. with the certain knowledge that she would get it. The adepts say they never waste energy, so they needed a spokesperson who would not require much effort to impress from afar.

H.P.B. was so good that she could clairvoyantly access documents in libraries she had never visited and accurately quote from pages of books there, translating them into English if necessary. Her explanation for this amazing achievement was that she read the passages "on another plane of existence." She would occasionally ask Olcott to check on a reference she had obtained clairvoyantly, and when he checked, he would discover that the page numbers were incorrect. If he reversed the numbers, however, he discovered that the reversed numbers gave the correct page. When he asked H.P.B. about it, she explained that when looking at something clairvoyantly it was similar to looking into a mirror. Everything was reversed. Because of that, she had to learn to read backward and then reverse the numbers. As might be expected, she occasionally forgot to reverse the numbers. Some years later, the same problem was noticed by associates who helped Blavatsky write *The Secret Doctrine*.

The second reason that H.P.B. may have been chosen as the Masters' agent is that she was thoroughly unselfish. Even her greatest enemies and those who regarded her as a fraud have never been able to charge her with selfishness. K.H. wrote to Sinnett that Blavatsky and Olcott "have that in them . . . which we have but too rarely found elsewhere—UNSELFISHNESS, and an eager readiness for self-sacrifice for the good of others; what a 'multitude of sins' does not this cover!" (ML, letter 131, p. 437). Examples of that unselfishness abound.

On January 6, 1889, the *New York Times* published an interview with William Q. Judge, a co-founder of the Theosophical Society. Judge had just returned from visiting H.P.B. in London. During the interview, Judge remarked that two prominent characteristics of Blavatsky were her energy and her great kindness. He said that some twelve years earlier, H.P.B. was traveling to New York from France. As she was about to board the ship, she noticed a woman with two small children. The woman was crying, so H.P.B. asked her why. Apparently the woman's husband had sent her money to pay for her and the children to sail to New York to join him there. Unfortunately, she had used all her money to buy a steerage class ticket for herself and children, only to discover that she had been swindled. The tickets were counterfeit. H.P.B. immediately exchanged her own first-class ticket for two steerage-class tickets, one for the woman and one for herself, so that the woman would not be left penniless and stranded in France (Olcott, *Old Diary Leaves* 1:28–29). Steerage passage at the time was a horror. There was almost no ventilation. It was overcrowded, and sanitary facilities were lacking. Moreover, one had to climb down a ladder to enter the steerage-class rooms. That alone was no small task for H.P.B. because she was overweight and not physically fit. One wonders how many people would have sacrificed their personal comfort just to do something so kind for a total stranger and suffered passage in steerage class rather than going first class. On another occasion while H.P.B was still in New York, Olcott reports that a Russian Orthodox priest came to the door to ask for alms for the poor. Blavatsky pointed to a drawer where she kept her money and said, "The money is in there. Take what you need."

In addition to Blavatsky's psychic ability and her unselfishness, she was loyal to her Teacher. Sometimes she would not be pleased with what he asked her to do, but she always carried out his directives. The adepts could count on her to follow through, no matter how difficult or unpleasant the task might be. During Blavatsky's talk with M. in 1851, she was told that she would get no personal benefit from the work she was asked to do. Her health was not particularly good and would not improve. She had little money and would get none from the work. Friends would betray her and she would be attacked by religious leaders of her day, and even by scientists who were convinced that reality consisted of little billiard-ball atoms with hard stuff as a nucleus. Nevertheless, Morya assured her that if she accepted the mission, she might be able to help people better understand themselves and the world in which they lived and, by using that knowledge, to relieve much of the suffering that is produced by actions taken in ignorance. She accepted the mission, and everything that Morya told her came true. She suffered from a kidney disorder; at her death she did not have enough money to pay for her funeral; friends betrayed her, causing her insufferable pain; and religious and scientific men attacked her as a devil worshiper or as a fraud.

One might wonder why the adepts chose the late 1800s to bring their ideas to the West and why they chose New York to launch their experiment. No one can say with certainty, but there are several compelling reasons that suggest the time was right. The first reason is that, in the early nineteenth century, western and central New York State was a hotbed of religious revival and new social ideas. A Protestant movement known as the Second Great Awakening was converting thousands of people, often at revival meetings. One aspect of the movement was to cure the ills of society before the second coming of Christ.

In addition to the Protestant revival, the area hosted a variety of new religious movements. One was the well-known Church of Jesus Christ of Latter-day Saints, commonly referred to as the Mormon Church. It began in the area with Joseph Smith, Jr., who believed that an angel led him to discover the Book of Mormon. Other movements were the Shakers and the Oneida Community, the latter promoting group marriage. Charles Grandison Finney, an abolitionist and a revivalist who favored social reforms to help African-Americans and women, called the whole area the "burned-over district" because there were hardly any unconverted people (fuel) to be converted (burned). In addition to the advent of new religious movements in the area, Elizabeth Cady Stanton, instrumental in establishing the Seneca Falls convention devoted to women's rights, suffrage among them, lived in Seneca Falls. Among the more liberal clergy, there were those who espoused the ideas in what came to be called the "Social Gospel," a movement that fought to overcome social ills such as alcoholism, crime, racial problems, child labor, and more.

Perhaps one of the greatest reasons the area was selected was because it was where Spiritualism began with the Fox sisters of Hydesville, New York. In the spring of 1848, the Fox sisters heard inexplicable knocks and rapping sounds around their home and tried to locate the source. To determine if a ghost was in the house and if that ghost could communicate with the living, their mother asked, "If you are a spirit, knock twice." In response, two loud knocks followed her question. Later investigation revealed that a man had been murdered in the house and his bones were discovered in the basement. The discovery led many in the country and in Europe to believe that the living could communicate with the dead. The popularity of the phenomena soon produced the Spiritualist Church, which taught that communion with the dead is possible. As might be expected, the possibility that life after death was provable excited a great many people who became convinced that they could communicate with deceased loved ones at séances. The craze spread rapidly, and soon New York City was overflowing with mediums, both real and fake, who promised they could contact deceased loved ones.

This new evidence for life beyond the grave contradicted materialistic nineteenth-century science, as well as religions that taught the dead were in purgatory, heaven, or hell. Apparently, although the dead were no longer in a physical body, they were here and could be reached through mediums. It was into this milieu of religious revival, new religious movements, social reform organizations, and Spiritualism that H. P. Blavatsky arrived in New York City in 1873.

In addition to this fertile ground for new thought and spiritual rebirth, New York City was fast becoming the fabled melting pot of humanity. People from every part of the globe and from every culture were already rubbing shoulders with one another in the city. Then as now, one could not walk more than a few blocks in the city without hearing at least two or three different languages. The adepts wanted their agents to encourage a realization of universal brotherhood, and there was probably no other place on earth where so many people from so many different traditions were living so close together on a relatively small island, the island of Manhattan. It was a promising place to begin the work.

One more important feature on the world stage in the late nineteenth century was the fact that religion and science were becoming more and more polar opposites. Science was entrenched in materialism, and despite new religious movements, the bulk of Protestant Christians were fundamentalists who believed that the Bible was literally the word of God. Those who could not accept a literal interpretation of scripture and who yet yearned for spiritual meaning were turning to Spiritualism by the thousands. There were mediums on practically every corner of major cities, just as today we might find tarot readers. The Masters wanted to counter the materialism of science and the superstition of religion.

In a letter to A. P. Sinnett, K.H. included an abridgement of a letter from the Chohan (Koot Hoomi's "boss"). That letter broached the Chohan's concern about the direction in which European society was headed. He wrote:

> The intellectual portions of mankind seem to be fast drifting into two classes, the one unconsciously preparing for itself long periods of temporary annihilation or states of non-consciousness, owing to the deliberate surrender of their intellect, its imprisonment in the narrow grooves of bigotry and superstition, a process which cannot fail to lead to the utter deformation of the intellectual principle; the other unrestrainedly indulging its animal propensities. . . . Between degrading superstition and still more degrading brutal materialism, the white dove of truth has hardly room where to rest her weary unwelcome foot. (LMW1:3–4)

By bringing their knowledge into the West, the Masters believed they could stem the tide of human degeneration, but they knew they could not do it instantly. In the same letter just quoted, the Chohan acknowledged the fact that "no prophet has ever achieved during his lifetime a complete triumph, not even Buddha." Yet, the Masters believed that they could supply spiritual meaning to those in search of it and that they could begin to bridge the gap between science and religion. As pointed out by the Chohan, the West was at a crossroad, one road leading to the suffocation of the human spirit through a materialist philosophy and the other road to superstition and religious bigotry. That being the case, the Masters stepped in to help. They searched for and found two individuals they thought could act as their agents in the West: H. P. Blavatsky, a Russian woman, and Henry Steel Olcott, an American. Morya wrote to Sinnett:

> So casting about we found in America the man to stand as leader—a man of great moral courage, unselfish, and having other good qualities. He was far from being the best, but (as Mr. Hume speaks in H.P.B.'s case)—he was the best one available. With him we associated a woman of most exceptional and wonderful endowments. Combined with them she had strong personal defects, but just as she was, there was no second to her living fit for this work. We sent her to America, brought them together—and the trial began. From the first both she and he were given to clearly understand that the issue lay entirely with themselves. And both offered themselves for the trial for certain remuneration in the far distant future—as K.H. would say—soldiers volunteer for a Forlorn Hope. (ML, letter 45, p. 125)

Olcott had been a colonel in the American Civil War, so Theosophists often refer to him as Colonel Olcott. He was also a lawyer, newspaper man, and agriculturalist. His first book, *Sor-*

ghum and Imphee, the Chinese and African Sugar Canes, became a school textbook. His reputation for integrity was so great that he was one of three men appointed to investigate the assassination of President Abraham Lincoln. He also rooted out corruption in the U. S. Grant presidential administration. Olcott was not a scientist, but he had a scientific mind. He based his beliefs on evidence rather than blind faith.

An example of Olcott's scientific approach took place in 1876 while he and H.P.B. were working on *Isis Unveiled*. They were seated opposite each other at a table in their New York apartment when they began to talk about certain occult principles. Olcott says that Blavatsky seemed unable to make her points clear to him, and, as usual, she accused him of being an idiot. Then, perhaps to illustrate a principle, H.P.B. took a small roll of white satin from a drawer, cut it to size, and laid it on the table, nearly covering it with a piece of paper. She rested her elbows on it and then rolled a cigarette for herself. Soon she asked Olcott to get her a drink of water. He agreed to get it but did not leave the table or take his eyes off of the satin. Blavatsky asked why he was waiting and he replied, "I only want to see what you are about to do with that satin." Blavatsky's temper flared. She brought her clenched fists down on the paper and said, "I shall have it now— this minute!" Then she tossed the satin to Olcott. On it was a "spirit picture" of the head only of Stainton Moses as he looked at that age, the almost duplicate of one of his photographs that hung on the wall of the room, over the mantel.

Olcott had remained in the room to make sure that Blavatsky

would not fool him. He wanted evidence even from his chum H.P.B. Olcott published a photo of the picture in *Old Diary Leaves* 1, opposite page 364, and it has been reproduced here.

Explaining in part why the adepts chose Olcott to work with Blavatsky, K.H. once summed up Olcott's character by writing:

Him we can trust under *all* circumstances, and his faithful service is pledged to us come well, come ill. . . . Where can we find an equal devotion? He is one who never questions, but obeys; who may make innumerable mistakes out of excessive zeal but never is unwilling to repair his fault even at the cost of the greatest self-humiliation; who esteems the sacrifice of comfort and even life something to be cheerfully risked whenever necessary; who will eat any food, or even go without; sleep on any bed, work in any place, fraternise with any outcast, endure any privation for the cause. (ML, letter 5, p. 17)

The Masters appear to have decided that 1875 was the right time and New York City the right place to launch their experiment. The stage had been set for the revelation of occult laws of nature that would lift a veil of ignorance and shine light on new hope for the redemption of humanity. That message was soon to be called "Theosophy."

After Blavatsky accepted the mission, Morya told her that he would have to train her for the work and that it would require her to be with him in Tibet for several years. In explanation of this, Blavatsky wrote:

True, there is no need of going absolutely to Tibet or India to find *some* knowledge and power "which are latent in every human soul"; but the acquisition of the highest knowledge and power requires not only many years of the severest study enlightened by a superior intelligence and an audacity bent by no peril; but also as many years of retreat in comparative solitude, and association with but students pursuing the same object, in a locality where nature itself preserves like the neophyte an absolute and unbroken stillness if not silence! Where the air is free for hundreds of miles around of all mephitic influence; the atmosphere and human magnetism absolutely pure and—no animal blood is spilt. (CW 3:268)

Some have doubted that a woman could have traveled alone to Tibet in the nineteenth century, but H.P.B. never said she went alone. Most likely, as an expert horsewoman, she went on horseback with at least one of her Teachers, either Morya or Koot Hoomi, both of whom were Indians, not Tibetans. There is no conclusive proof that H.P.B. spent time in Tibet, but neither is there any evidence that she did not. The question must remain open.

Although the adepts chose Blavatsky as their agent, she was not an adept. In fact, K.H. reported that, although she was their direct agent, she was not a true chela. *Chela* is a term used by the adepts to refer to a student who is closely linked to them and who is on the way to becoming an adept. That seems a strange situation, but her strong passionate nature and personality made adeptship impossible in that incarnation. Nevertheless, the adepts had the highest praise for her.

Since the late nineteenth century, when H. P. Blavatsky introduced Morya and Koot Hoomi to the West, there has been a great deal of speculation about them. Are they living men or figments of Blavatsky's imagination? If they are living men, what distinguishes them from ordinary people?

Chapter 2

THE MAHATMAS: WHAT ARE THEY? WHO ARE THEY?

Before we consult the Mahatma Letters to learn what the Mahatmas have to say about what distinguishes them from ordinary persons, we can consider the logical necessity of there being highly developed human beings who are geniuses in intellect and spiritual giants in their inner self, and then define what aspect of our human nature is denoted by the term *inner self*.

If we accept the possibility of life beyond physical death, and if we accept the possibility of reincarnation, then it follows that our experiences in each incarnation will teach us something about life and human relations. Even if we do not accept the possibility of reincarnation, it is obvious that people around us are in different stages of human development. Some are intellectually gifted, while others are not. Some have amazing artistic ability, and others cannot draw a stick figure accurately. Some have great sensitivity and an extraordinary ability in the field of human relations; others do not. We can explain such differences as the result of continual learning through reincarnation. It then seems inevitable that at some point individuals can become *adepts*— that is, fully developed human beings. Of course, this is but theory for most of us, but it is not an unreasonable theory. With that theory in mind, we can consult the Mahatma Letters and the primary source material from Blavatsky to learn how she and the Mahatmas define *mahatma*.

The introductory notes (p. xvii) of the Mahatma Letters include a quotation from Blavatsky explaining what a mahatma is. She writes:

A Mahatma is a personage who, by special training and education, has evolved those higher faculties and has attained that spiritual knowledge which ordinary humanity will acquire after passing through numberless series of incarnations.

K.H. adds to that definition by writing:

The adept is the rare efflorescence of a generation of enquirers; and to become one, he must obey the inward impulse of his soul irrespective of the prudential considerations of worldly science or sagacity. (ML, letter 2, p. 6)

Blavatsky reports that the Mahatmas are members of an occult brotherhood and that most of them live in Tibet. She tells us that while they can live for hundreds of years, none of them is thousands of years old. Of Morya, her own Master, she wrote that she did not know how old he was, but when she first met him in her twenties he was in "the very prime of manhood." Now, she added, "I am an old woman, but he has not aged a day" (CW 8:400).

In an interview published in the *New York Sun*, May 6, 1877, in response to the reporter's question about the number of adepts, H.P.B. responded that there were at least one to two thousand adepts living at her time. She said:

[There are] several thousand [Adepts], nearly all in the East. Perhaps there are half a dozen Adepts in Europe. I have not met any in this country [the United States]. There are a few Adepts in Central and South America. (Gomes, *Dawning of the Theosophical Movement*, p. 8)

H.P.B. was known to exaggerate, so perhaps the number was more likely in the hundreds than in the thousands.

In his first letter to A. O. Hume (of the National Indian Congress), K.H. writes that the number of adepts is diminishing. He explains:

The cycles must run their rounds. Periods of mental and moral light and darkness succeed each other, as day does night. The major and minor yugas [one of the four ages of the Hindu world cycle] must be accomplished according to the established order of things. And we, borne along on the mighty tide, can only modify and direct some of its minor currents. . . . True also, our numbers are just now diminishing but this is because, as I have said, we are of the human race, subject to its cyclic impulse and powerless to turn that back upon itself. (ML, appendix 1, p. 474)

Blavatsky claimed to have met a number of adepts in addition to the two who became her Teachers and who inspired what became the Theosophical Society. She claimed to have met the European Master Hilarion in Greece and to have studied with other Masters in Syria and Egypt. Among those known to her was Serapis Bey, a member of another occult brotherhood known as the Hermetic Brotherhood of Luxor. C. Jinarajadasa published seventeen letters from Serapis to Olcott in *Letters from the Masters of the Wisdom*, Second Series (LMW2:11–49). K.H. verifies the existence of other Masters and claims that they organize into various brotherhoods. He writes:

There are even at the present moment three centres of the Occult Brotherhood in existence, widely separated geographically, and as widely exoterically—the true esoteric doctrine being identical in substance though differing in terms; all aiming at the same grand object, but no two agreeing seemingly in the details of procedure. (ML, letter 120, p. 410)

Although different Masters have come through different religious traditions, K.H. and Morya consider themselves to be

Buddhist. They are not *exoteric* Buddhists, however, because they do not practice popular Buddhist rites, nor do they accept the superstition that inevitably creeps into all religions, including Buddhism.

> The Masters are living, human beings. They are not disembodied spirits, and despite their extraordinary powers, they are neither omniscient nor omnipotent. K.H. commented on that when he wrote to Sinnett: *"We are not infallible, all-foreseeing 'Mahatmas' at every hour of the day."* (ML, letter 136, p. 450)

When centered in brain consciousness, they are, as K.H. once said, ordinary men. Just as there are many degrees of development among us ordinary mortals, there are degrees of development among our elder Brothers. K.H. speaks of recently having attained a *"higher"* light" and then adds, "and even that one, in no wise the most dazzling to be acquired on this earth. Verily the *Light of Omniscience* and infallible Prevision on this earth . . . is yet far away from me!" (ML, letter 117, p. 400).

The very idea of mahatmas, masters, adepts, or "the Brothers" as they were often called, was new to the West when H.P.B. began to talk about her Teachers in the late nineteenth century. As a result, there was a great deal of curiosity about them. A. P. Sinnett was especially curious, and at one point evidently asked K.H. to explain what differentiated an adept from the ordinary person. In letter 85B, K.H. replied:

(1) An adept—the highest as the lowest—is one *only during the exercise of his occult powers.* (2) Whenever these powers are needed, the sovereign will unlock the door to the *inner* man (the adept). . . . (3) The smallest exercise of occult powers then, as you will now see, requires an effort. We may compare it to the inner muscular effort of an athlete preparing to use his physical strength. As no athlete is likely to be always amusing himself at swelling his veins in anticipation of having to lift a weight, so no adept can be supposed to keep his will in constant tension and the *inner* man in full function, when there is no immediate necessity for it. When the *inner* man rests the adept becomes an ordinary man, limited to his physical senses and the functions of his physical brain. Habit sharpens the intuition of the latter, yet is unable to make them supersensuous. The inner adept is ever ready, ever on the alert, and that suffices for our purposes. At moments of rest then, his faculties are at rest also. When I sit at my meals, or when I am dressing, reading or otherwise occupied I am not thinking even of those near me; and Djual Khool [a student of K.H. living nearby] can easily break his nose to blood, by running in the dark against a beam, as he did the other night . . . and I remained placidly ignorant of the fact. *I was not thinking of him*—hence my ignorance. From the aforesaid, you may well infer that an adept is an ordinary mortal at all moments of his daily life but those—when the *inner* man is acting. . . . K.H. when writing to us *is not an adept.* A *non-*adept—is fallible. There-

fore, K.H. may very easily commit mistakes;—Mistakes of punctuation—that will often change entirely the whole sense of a sentence; idiomatic mistakes—very likely to occur, especially when writing as hurriedly as I do. (ML, letter 85B, pp. 257–258)

As further testimony to his being a mortal, K.H. wrote: "Meanwhile, being *human* I have to rest. I took no sleep for over 60 hours" (ML, letter 12, p. 39).

From what K.H. says, it should be clear that the Masters are not miracle workers. He told Sinnett: "The wiseacres say: 'The age of miracles is past,' but we answer, 'It never existed!'" (ML, letter 12, p. 38). The adepts report that they work by following natural, not supernatural, law and that all of their remarkable powers are latent abilities in every human being. It took them many lives to reach their goal, but they claim that

there comes a moment in the life of an adept, when the hardships he has passed through are a thousandfold rewarded. In order to acquire further knowledge, he has no more to go through a minute and slow process of investigation and comparison of various objects, but is accorded an instantaneous, implicit insight into every first truth. (ML, letter 17, p. 55)

Many in the Theosophical movement have tended to put the Masters on a pedestal as though they were gods. K.H. noted this early on and remarked on it to Sinnett when he wrote:

For years to come the Soc. will be unable to stand, when based upon "Tibetan Brothers" and phenomena alone. . . . There is a hero-worshipping tendency clearly showing itself, and you, my friend, are not quite free from it yourself. . . . If you would go on with your occult studies and literary work—then learn to be loyal to the Idea, rather than to my poor self. . . . I am far from being perfect. (ML, letter 130, pp. 432–433)

The Masters are not omnipotent. Blavatsky reports: "The highest Adept, put into a new Body, has to struggle against and subdue it, and finds its subjugation difficult" (CW 12:692).

The struggle of the inner self against the outer body has been known and spoken of for centuries. The Gospel of St. Matthew (26:41) tells us that "the spirit indeed is willing but the flesh is weak," and those struggling to live a spiritual life experience a war within themselves between the spirit and the flesh, between the inner will and temptations arising in the body and the personality. H.P.B. tells us that the fundamental reason for this struggle comes from what she calls a "triple evolutionary scheme" of the body, the mind, and the spirit. The physical body has its impulses, the mind has its conditioned responses, and the spirit tries to subjugate both mind and body to bring them into harmony with its own sovereign will.

An adept is an individual who is functioning from his own inner self and not from brain consciousness or from what we call "the personality." The inner self may be the state of consciousness that St. Paul calls "Christ Jesus" when he says: "There is neither Jew nor Greek, there is neither bond nor free, there is neither male nor female: for ye are all one in Christ Jesus" (Galatians 3:28). In Theosophy, that state is called "buddhi," and it is said to be a state of universal consciousness.

When H.P.B. first spoke of the Brothers as her Teachers, she aroused a great deal of curiosity about them. In addition to Brothers, she often called her Teachers "Masters," and perhaps that word led many to believe that the Brothers were godlike men. To Blavatsky, the word *masters* simply meant "teachers," as in schoolmasters. With little understanding of what an adept was, people began to treat the Masters much like Christian saints who can be petitioned for help. H.P.B. considered it a desecration of the Masters to assume that they would help individuals with their personal affairs. In one of her letters, published in the March/April 1982 issue of *The Eclectic Theosophist*, she wrote, "Dozens of times I have declared that I *shall not* put the Masters any worldly questions or submit before Them family and other private matters, personal for the most part."

The rejection of personal requests was emphasized again in a letter that K.H. wrote to Annie Besant in 1900:

The cant about "Masters" must be silently but firmly put down. Let the devotion and service be to that Supreme Spirit alone of which each one is a part. Namelessly and silently we work and the continual references to ourselves and the repetition of our names raises up a confused aura that hinders our work. (LMW1:100)

The "confused aura" is the aura of thought. Few realize that "thoughts are things—have tenacity, coherence, and life,—that they are real entities" (ML, letter 18, p. 66). K.H. explains that

> every thought of man . . . becomes an active entity by associating itself . . . with an elemental; that is to say with one of the semi-intelligent forces of the kingdoms. It survives as an active intelligence, a creature of the mind's begetting, for a longer or shorter period proportionate with the original intensity of the cerebral action which generated it. Thus, a good thought is perpetuated as an active beneficent power; an evil one as a maleficent demon. And so man is continually peopling his current in space with a world of his own, crowded with the offspring of his fancies, desires, impulses, and passions, a current which reacts upon any sensitive or . . . nervous organization which comes in contact with it. . . . the Adept evolves these shapes consciously, other men throw them off unconsciously. (ML, appendix 1, p. 472)

Most of us have had the experience of thinking of a friend and within seconds getting a phone call from him or her. It is the thought from our friend that has impressed itself upon our mind. Imagine how thoughts from thousands of people might affect one as sensitive as an adept. It then becomes easy to understand how those thoughts would set up a "confused aura."

Because of the confused aura of thought that gets in the way of their work, the adepts do not want to have anyone prove that they exist. K.H. wrote to Sinnett:

And I wish I could impress upon your minds the deep conviction that we do not wish Mr. Hume or you to prove conclusively to the public that we really exist. Please realize the fact that so long as men doubt there will be curiosity and enquiry, and that enquiry stimulates reflection which begets effort; but let our secret be once thoroughly vulgarized and not only will skeptical society derive no great good but our privacy would be constantly endangered and have to be continually guarded at an unreasonable cost of power. (ML, letter 29, p. 93)

In an earlier letter K.H. told Sinnett that "the charlatans and the jugglers are the natural shields of the 'adepts'" (ML, letter 1, p. 4). That may seem a strange thing to say, but consider the fact that the abundance of charlatans makes well-educated people doubt that there could be any such thing as Masters or occult power. Such ideas would be dismissed as superstitious nonsense by intellectually gifted but often morally impure people who would seek out the Masters with their powerful but selfish thoughts. Focused and powerful thoughts coming from highly developed minds would be a greater problem for the adepts than feeble thoughts from those whose mental development is not so great.

Although the Masters do not get involved with individuals in any personal way, they do work with individuals who can be helpful in the great work for humanity. If they notice an individual who is struggling to do something useful for mankind, they may influence that person by planting an idea in their mind in the hope that the individual will pick up on it and carry the idea through to fruition. The individual so influenced may never know that their brilliant idea came from one of the Masters.

When working with individuals, even their closest students, they never force them to follow orders. Morya wrote to Sinnett: "We *advise*—and never *order*. But we *do* influence individuals" (ML, letter 49, p. 134). By "influence," the adept most likely means that he will send a positive thought about the best course of action for the student. Perhaps he might even influence a scientist who is on the verge of an important discovery, prodding him in a direction that will clarify his thought on the subject. The way the individual responds to that influence is entirely up to the individual. In a later letter to Sinnett, K.H. wrote: "The fact is, that to the last and supreme initiation every chela—(and even some adepts)—is left to his own device and counsel" (ML, letter 92, p. 294). To force someone to do something, the adept would have to override the will of the subject with his own more powerful will, and that is something the adepts say they never do. K.H. comments on that when he writes that the adepts "are forbidden by our wise and intransgressible laws to completely subject to themselves another and a weaker will,—that of free born man. The latter mode of proceeding is the favourite one resorted to by the 'Brothers of the Shadow,' the Sorcerers, the Elementary Spooks" (ML, letter 18, p. 59). Theoretically, the effects of karma always rebound on the one who originates an action. It follows that, should an adept demand that his students do something, the results would rebound more on the adept than on the student. K.H. wrote to C. W. Leadbeater: "If

I were to *demand* that you should do one thing or the other, instead of simply advising, I would be responsible for every effect that might flow from the step and you acquire but a secondary merit" (LMW1:29).

K.H. makes a curious statement that suggests we can know him only as we know others, that is, as an ordinary mortal. We cannot know him as an adept. He writes:

For you know—or think you know, of *one* K.H.—and can know but of one, whereas there are two distinct personages answering to that name *in him* you know. The riddle is only apparent and easy to solve, were you only to know what a real *Mahatma* is. (ML, letter 130, p. 433)

Clearly the one K.H. that we can know is the personal K.H., the man of flesh and blood. Being flesh-and-blood men, K.H. and Morya could be distinguished from each other just as any two people can be. Over the years, a number of alleged photographs and portraits of Master K.H. and Master Morya have appeared, most of them having little or no resemblance to the real Masters. There are portraits of K.H. and Morya, however, that H.P.B. verified as valid. Those portraits were painted by the German artist Hermann Schmiechen between June 19 and July 9, 1884, in London while the founders were there. Blavatsky described the adepts to the artist and, when they were completed, said that the portrait of Morya was "a good likeness" and that the one of K.H. was a good likeness in features, but that K.H. was lighter in complexion than the artist had painted him.

Commenting on the proposed portraits, Morya wrote: "I myself will guide his hands with brush for K's portrait" (LMW1:158). When K.H. mentioned his own portrait to Sinnett, he said, "I believe you are now satisfied with my portrait made by Herr Schmiechen and as dissatisfied with the one you have? Yet all are like in their way. Only while the others are the productions of chelas, the last one was painted with M.'s hand on the artist's head, and often on his arm" (ML, letter 129, p. 430). Those original portraits now hang in the shrine room of the Theosophical Society in Adyar, Chennai, India. They were reproduced in Manly P. Hall's 1931 illustrated journal, *The Phoenix*, and they are reproduced here.

MASTER K.H. AND MASTER MORYA

Like all of us, the adepts have personalities, and from all we can gather from their letters and from those few people who had direct contact with them, K.H. and Morya had very different personalities.

When K.H. and Morya decided to help Westerners understand something of their philosophy, K.H. decided that he should live and study with Europeans for a while. K.H. was not then a full adept but rather a highly developed student well on his way to that goal. Apparently he thought that the only way he could get an accurate picture of the Western mind was to spend some time with Westerners. H.P.B. reports that K.H. traveled a good deal in Europe (CW 8:398), where he has been reported to have attended Trinity College in Dublin and a university in Germany. While we have no evidence for that, K.H. did acknowledge that he had "a bit of Western education" (ML, letter 136, p. 450) and in one of his letters wrote, "And which of our holy Shaberons [roughly, great adepts] has had the benefit of even the little university education and inkling of European manners that has fallen to my share?" (ML, letter 5, p. 18). As a result of his stay in Europe, K.H. learned to speak fluent English and French. In fact, Morya called him "my Frenchified K.H." (ML, letter 26, p. 84).

K.H. writes well in English, although at times he is a bit verbose. Often, he expresses himself in poetic language worthy of some of our great poets. In one case, after he had returned from what was described as a long retreat, K.H. wrote to Sinnett:

> My Brother—I have been on a long journey after supreme knowledge, I took a long time to rest. Then, upon coming back, I had to give all my time to duty, and all my thoughts to the Great Problem. It is all over now: the New Year's festivities are at an end and I am "Self" once more. But what is *Self*? Only a passing guest, whose concerns are all like a mirage of the great desert. (ML, letter 47, p. 129)

K.H. has a kind and loving nature; yet, like Morya, he speaks frankly. If he wants to help a friend by pointing out a weakness he or she needs to overcome, he will try to be gentle about it, using such phrases as "I hope I will not hurt your feelings if I say. . . ." This is in stark contrast to Morya, who although still loving, tends to be blunt in such matters. Once K.H. wrote to Sinnett that Morya is

> as stern for himself, as severe for his own shortcomings, as he is indulgent for the defects of other people . . . yet [he] was ever a stauncher friend to you than myself, who may often hesitate to hurt anyone's feelings, even in speaking the strictest truth. (ML, letter 74, p. 224)

K.H. appreciates music and the fine arts. In fact, he regards music as "the most divine and *spiritual* of arts" (ML, letter 85B, p. 264). A few times, while Sinnett was playing some of Beethoven's waltzes, K.H. was listening in, not physically, but from a distance by being in rapport with Sinnett and his music. As a consequence, K.H. asked a favor of Sinnett. He wrote:

> You, my good friend, whom I had once or twice the pleasure of hearing playing on your piano . . . tell me, could you favour me as readily as with one of your easy *waltzes*—with one of Beethoven's Grand Sonatas? (ML, letter 68, p. 202)

Only the highest adepts can free themselves totally from earthly connections and from "the higher pleasures, emotions, and interests of the common run of humanity." K.H. confesses that he is not yet free from some earthly attractions. He writes:

> I am still attracted towards *some* men more than toward others, and philanthropy . . . has never killed in me either individual preferences of friendship, love for my next of kin, or the ardent feeling of patriotism for the country in which I was last materially individualized. (ML, letter 15, p. 49)

Among their personal traits is a keen sense of humor and common sense. Blavatsky is reported to have said that the most important quality for the spiritual life is common sense. When pressed for the second most important, she said "a sense of humor." That is reasonable because humor is based on the incongruous, and in order to know what is incongruous, we must know what is congruous. The adepts know that well, and their sense of humor comes through in their letters. Once when K.H.

was growing tired of Sinnett's unending questions, he wrote: "And now, how long do you propose to abstain from interrogation marks?" (ML, letter 68, p. 202). On another occasion when he had just witnessed an avalanche and was taking advantage of the awful stillness following it, he got a rude shock from H.P.B. He wrote:

> But just as I was taking advantage of the awful stillness which usually follows such cataclysm . . . I was rudely recalled to my senses. A familiar voice, as shrill as the one attributed to Saraswati's peacock—which, if we may credit tradition, frightened off the King of the Nagas—shouted along the currents "Olcott has raised the very devil again! . . . The Englishmen are going crazy. . . . Koot Hoomi, *come quicker* and help me!"—and in her excitement forgot she was speaking English. I must say, that the "Old Lady's" telegrams do strike one like stones from a catapult! (ML, letter 5, p. 15)

In contrast to K.H., Morya does not enjoy writing letters, and when he does he uses a minimum of words. K.H. reports that "'M' knows very little English and *hates* writing" (ML, letter 66, p. 175). Once when writing to Sinnett, Morya said he used "the best English I find lying idle in my friend's [K.H.'s] brain" (ML, letter 42, p. 112). Despite his dislike of writing, when K.H. was on his retreat, M. promised him that he would watch over his work, and he took on the unpleasant task of answering letters that would ordinarily have been answered by K.H. When Morya wrote a particularly long letter to Sinnett, he said, "I close the longest letter I have ever written in my life; but as I do it for K.H.—I am satisfied" (ML, letter 29, p. 94).

Sinnett called Morya "an imperious sort of chap," and K.H. acknowledged the fact when he wrote:

> I am prepared to concede . . . that he [Morya] is *a very imperious* sort of chap, and certainly very apt *sometimes* to become angry, especially if he is opposed in what he knows to be right. Would you think more of him, were he to *conceal* his anger; to *lie* to himself and the outsiders, and so permit them to credit him with a virtue he has not? (ML, letter 74, p. 224)

While defending H.P.B. against attacks on her personality, K.H. once told Sinnett of an amusing incident involving Morya and his angry response to something Blavatsky did. He wrote:

> She is given to exaggeration in general, and when it becomes a question of "puffing up" those she is devoted to, her enthusiasm knows no limits. Thus she has made of M. an Apollo of Belvedere, the glowing description of whose physical beauty made him more than once start in anger, and break his pipe while swearing like a true—Christian; and thus, under her eloquent phraseology, I myself had the pleasure of hearing myself metamorphosed into an "angel of purity and light"— shorn of his wings. We cannot help feeling at times angry with, oftener—laughing at, her. Yet the feeling that dictates

all this ridiculous effusion is too ardent, too sincere and true, not to be respected or even treated with indifference. (ML, letter 92, p. 297)

Morya's sense of humor often comes out as irony. A clear example of that irony is in a letter that M. wrote to one of his students in response to a letter informing him that the student was a member of a secret organization. The student assumed that M. would know all about it. He did not. Morya replied:

Two or three sentences [in your letter] . . . are well calculated to make even an *adept* scratch his head. Especially solemn and mysterious is the one that begins with "As you know, my Father, I belong, etc.," and referring to a certain secret society. This news that you belong (besides the Theos.) to another "Society of . . ." in which no one member knows the other, and one that *neither practices nor tolerates deceit*—filled me with awe and admiration, no less than that other piece of news that informed me that some of its members claimed to know and communicate with me. Alas! notwithstanding your assurance—"as you (I) know"—I confess to my great shame, that I know very little of it—probably owing to your usual precaution. Hitherto, you had locked it up so safely in a remote corner of your brain, and "composed your mind" so well when writing to me, that of course I was unable to get at it. Yes; we know little of it; too grand and respectable for us, altogether, notwithstanding the acquaintance claimed. And since regardless of its *carbonari*-like character, that precludes the possibility of one member knowing any other member, you still seem to know *several* of them who claim to know and hold relations with me—I must naturally infer that you are very high in it—its President perhaps, the "High Venerable Master"? (LMW2:142–143)

Even though M. had rebuked the student sternly, he wanted him to know that he still cared for him, so he ended that letter by saying, "Yours still lovingly, M∴"

Stories about the personal side of the Masters include an amusing incident with a goat. While K.H. was with a friend at a monastery near Phari-Johg in Tibet, he received a packet containing a letter from Sinnett and one from a Theosophist by the name of C. C. Massey. K.H. told Sinnett that he was "busy with important affairs" and did not have time to read the letters. After opening the "thick packet" that contained the letters, he merely glanced at them and, he thought, slipped them into his traveling bag. What he did not realize was that the letters had dropped on the ground. Soon he heard a young man "calling out from a window, and expostulating with someone at a distance." As K.H. turned around, he understood what the commotion was all about. There was an old goat making a meal of the letters. It had already devoured part of the letter from Massey, "and was thoughtfully preparing to have a bite at yours [Sinnett's], more delicate and easy for chewing with his old teeth than the tough envelope and paper of your correspondent's epistle." In spite of strong opposition and disgust from the animal, it took K.H. but an instant to rescue what was left of the letters.

The Masters have very strict rules about using psychic power, and K.H. reported that he *"had no right to restore"* the letters because the rule "forbids our using one minim of power until every ordinary means has been tried and failed" (ML, letter 68, p. 203). Therefore, he resolved to speak to the Chohan (his superior), to ask for permission to restore the letters when he heard the voice of the Chohan saying, "Why break the rule? I will do it myself," and he did. K.H. says he thanked the goat heartily and, to show his gratitude, "strengthened what remained of teeth in his mouth . . . so that he may chew food harder than English letters for several years yet to come" (ML, letter 92, p. 303).

Chapter 3

EARLY LETTERS

THE FADEYEV LETTER

The first letter we know of that was written by an adept is one to Blavatsky's aunt, Nadya Fadeyev. The letter was written in French on rice paper used in Kashmir and Punjab but not common in Europe. It was written in the handwriting of K.H. and received in 1870, a full five years before the founding of the Theosophical Society in New York.

Unknown to her family, H.P.B. had been in Tibet for some time and no one was able to locate her. Naturally, the family was very worried about her and thought perhaps she might be dead. Then, probably in November 1870, Nadya received K.H.'s letter assuring her that her niece was well and happy. The letter did not come by ordinary post but, according to Nadya, was delivered in a most startling way. She described the receipt of the letter to Olcott and promised to send him the letter in case it might be useful. She wrote: "I received a letter from him, whom I believe you call "K.H.," which was brought to me in the most incomprehensible and mysterious manner, by a messenger of Asiatic appearance, who then disappeared before my very eyes" (Cranston, *HPB*, pp. 102–103). The letter informed Nadya that her niece was at a "distant and unknown retreat" she had selected for herself, but that she would return home in about eighteen months.

THE FIRST LETTER TO A. P. SINNETT

Like many others, Sinnett had been fascinated with the occult phenomena he had witnessed. He was convinced that it was valid, and he wanted to prove to the world, especially to the skeptics, that forces beyond those known by scientists were real. Therefore, he devised what he thought would be a foolproof test that would convince even the most hardened skeptic. He described the experiment he had in mind in a letter to "An Unknown Master," and gave the letter to H.P.B. to transmit. Sinnett asked the "Unknown Master" to produce one day's edition of the London *Times* and *The Pioneer* simultaneously in Simla. *The Pioneer* was an English-language newspaper published in India, and in the 1880s, communication between London and India took about a month. The telegraph existed then, but to telegraph the entire *Times* to India and have it published on the same day was an impossible task. Therefore, Sinnett was convinced that this test would silence the skeptics forever.

About October 15, 1880, Sinnett received a reply from K.H., and the contents of that letter must have come as a shock to him. K.H. wrote:

> Precisely because the test of the London newspaper would close the mouths of the skeptics—it is unthinkable . . . and the results would be deplorable. . . . [They] would prove very soon a trap. (ML, letter 1, pp. 1–2)

K.H. went on to explain that those who would regard the phenomenon as valid would attribute it to the "dark agencies" that about two thirds of humanity believed in and dreaded. Sinnett had said that "half London would be converted," but K.H. replied that "if the people believed the thing true they would kill you before you could make the round of Hyde Park; if it were not believed true, the least that could happen would be the loss of your reputation and good name—for propagating such ideas." Some scientists and the less superstitious public who believed the phenomenon valid would require test after test, and "every subsequent phenomenon expected to be more marvelous than the preceding one" (ML, letter 1, pp. 2, 3). The Master added that "the higher and educated classes would go on disbelieving as ever, tearing you to shreds as before . . . [and] so long as science has anything to learn, and a shadow of religious dogmatism lingers in the hearts of the multitudes, the world's prejudices have to be conquered step by step, not at a rush" (ML, letter 1, p. 4).

The correspondence between Sinnett and the Mahatmas

went on to include more than a hundred and forty letters. Koot Hoomi, Morya, and some of the other adepts also corresponded with a few select Westerners and Easterners, including A. O. Hume, Olcott, and a number of people involved in the Theosophical movement. Many of these letters are in the collection compiled by C. Jinarajadasa in his two-volume work, *Letters from the Masters of the Wisdom.* The last letter we know that K.H. sent was to Mrs. Besant, the second international president of the Theosophical Society. It was sent in 1900. So far as anyone knows, that letter ended the correspondence.

Chapter 4

GOD, EVIL, AND
OCCULT PHILOSOPHY

Blavatsky never claimed that the Mahatma Letters and her own writings contained final wisdom. Rather, she said that Theosophy had not solved the mysteries of the universe. It had merely lifted a corner of the veil. The Masters gave out what little of the occult doctrine as they thought might be useful.

Sinnett was a veritable question mark when it came to pushing for occult information. In response to his overenthusiastic requests, K.H. told him:

The Occult Science is *not* one in which secrets can be communicated of a sudden, by a written or even verbal communication. If so, all the "Brothers" would have to do, would be to publish a *Hand-book* of the art which might be taught in schools as grammar is. It is the common mistake of people that we willingly wrap ourselves and our powers in mystery—

that we wish to keep our knowledge to ourselves, and of our own will refuse—"wantonly and deliberately" to communicate it. The truth is that till the neophyte attains to the condition necessary for that degree of Illumination to which, and for which, he is entitled and fitted, most *if not all* of the Secrets are *incommunicable*. The receptivity must be equal to the desire to instruct. The illumination *must come from within*. Till then no hocus pocus of incantations, or mummery of appliances, no metaphysical lectures or discussions, no self-imposed penance can give it. All these are but means to an end, and all we can do is to direct the use of such means as have been empirically found by the experience of ages to conduce to the required object. And this was and has been *no secret* for thousands of years. Fasting, meditation, chastity of thought, word, and deed; silence for certain periods of time to enable nature herself to speak to him who comes to her for information; government of the animal passions and impulses; utter unselfishness of intention, the use of certain incense and fumigations for physiological purposes, have been published as the means since the days of Plato and Iamblichus in the West and since the far earlier times of our Indian *Rishis*. (ML, letter 20, pp. 72–73)

DOES GOD EXIST?

In *The Secret Doctrine*, Blavatsky sums up a few points she believes she has proven. In the first two points, H.P.B. clarifies her position, and undoubtedly the position of the Masters, on the question of atheism. She writes:

> (1) The Secret Doctrine teaches no *Atheism*, except in the Hindu sense of the word *nastika*, or the rejection of *idols*, including every anthropomorphic god. In this sense every Occultist is a *Nastika*. (2) It admits a Logos or a collective "Creator" of the Universe; a *Demiurgos*—in the sense implied when one speaks of an "Architect" as the "Creator" of an edifice, whereas that Architect has never touched one stone of it, but, while furnishing the plan, left all the manual labour to the masons; in our case the plan was furnished by the Ideation of the Universe, and the constructive labour was left to the Hosts of intelligent Powers and Forces. But that *Demiurgos* is no *personal* deity,—i.e., an imperfect *extra-cosmic god*,—but only the aggregate of the Dhyan-Chohans and the other forces. (SD 1:279–280)

Some have charged the adepts and the founders of the Theosophical Society with prejudice against Christianity. The fact is, however, that they have not only criticized what they believe to be error and superstition in Christianity, but also in Vedantism, Buddhism, and Hinduism in its various branches. K.H. reports that they are impartial to Christianity, not hostile to it (ML, letter 92, p. 300).

K.H. claims that the Jesus of the New Testament is a "spiritual abstraction" rather than a "living man of that epoch" (ML, letter 38, p. 109). He differentiates between the Christ and the

man Jesus by saying that the former is the sixth principle of
the human being, buddhi. He claims that the human Jesus was
"an adept more by his inherent purity and ignorance of real
Evil than by what he had learned with his initiated Rabbis and
the already . . . fast degenerating Egyptian Hierophants and
priests" (ML, letter 111, p. 377). According to K.H., it was not
only Jesus who was an adept, but Paul, whom he calls "the Christian Adept, the Kabalistic Paul [who said]: 'Know ye not that ye
are the temple of God *and that the Spirit of God dwelleth in you*'"
(ML, letter 111, p. 377).

There can be no doubt that the adepts reject the idea of any
extra-cosmic god, including the one portrayed by exoteric Judaism, Christianity, and Islam. They do not deny there are great
truths in the scriptures. Occasionally they even quote a passage
from the Bible that they believe illustrates a point they are making. They reject a literal interpretation of everything in the Bible,
however, and they do not believe that every word of it is divinely
inspired. As to the idea of an individual spirit and personal God,
K.H. writes: "Neither our philosophy nor ourselves believe in a
God, least of all in one whose pronoun necessitates a capital H"
(ML, letter 88, p. 269). He goes on to state:

> The idea of God is not an innate but an acquired notion. . . .
> The God of the Theologians is simply an imaginary power . . .
> a power which has never yet manifested itself. Our chief aim
> is to deliver humanity of this nightmare, to teach man virtue
> for its own sake, and to walk in life relying on himself instead

of leaning on a theological crutch, that for countless ages was the direct cause of nearly all human misery. Pantheistic we may be called—agnostic NEVER. K.H. then says that if people want to call "our ONE LIFE" God, then they may do so, but it will be a "gigantic misnomer." (ML, letter 88, p. 270)

It may seem overstated to say that "nearly all human misery" has been caused by religion, but a look at history reveals that the statement is not far from the truth. Religious wars have been going on throughout recorded history. Furthermore, most if not all of the various cultures around the world have arisen out of one religion or another. Even though a majority of people in any given culture have ceased to believe what their theologians teach, cultural clashes persist and wars result. Fanatical belief has caused families to split apart and neighbors to turn against neighbors. Both individually and nationally, religion has caused a great deal of human misery. At the same time, much good has come from religious teaching. Christianity, for example, is responsible for encouraging care of the poor and establishing charitable institutions around the world, and all major religions teach compassion. Unfortunately, the teaching often falls on deaf ears.

K.H. calls the idea of a personal God a nightmare because a nightmare is imaginary. It exists only in the mind of the one experiencing the nightmare, and it is a frightening experience. God is to be feared, say those who believe in the God portrayed in the Bible, and for centuries many have been terrified of God's potential wrath against them. Fortunately, this seems less so in recent years, but there are still those who are afraid that they will be sent to an eternal hell of punishment for what sometimes seem to be only minor infractions.

Even though mainstream Christianity has a somewhat less anthropomorphic view of God today, the church still teaches that the God of the Bible is omniscient, omnipotent, and full of love. K.H. challenges that view by asking Sinnett how he can believe such a doctrine "when everything in nature, physical and moral, proves such a being, if he does exist, to be quite the reverse of all you say of him." He adds, "Strange delusion and one which seems to overpower your very intellect" (ML, letter 90, p. 282).

Despite their rejection of an extra-cosmic personal deity, the adepts are intellectually honest. K.H. writes:

> You were told that our knowledge was limited to this our solar system: ergo as philosophers who desired to remain worthy of the name we could not either deny or affirm the existence of what you termed a supreme, omnipotent, intelligent being of some sort *beyond* the limits of that solar system. But if such an existence is not absolutely impossible, yet unless the uniformity of nature's law breaks at those limits we maintain that it is highly improbable. (ML, letter 88, p. 270)

Nevertheless, the Masters know that the God the Bible says can be angry, jealous, and even vindictive does not exist in our solar system.

In 1705, Samuel Clarke published *A Demonstration of the Being and Attributes of God*. K.H. was obviously aware of Clarke's "proofs" of God's existence and commented on the following "proof" to Sinnett:

> "God who hath made the eye, shall not see? God who hath made the ear shall he not hear?" But according to this mode of reasoning they would have to admit that in creating an idiot God is an idiot; that he who made so many irrational beings, so many physical and moral monsters, must be an irrational being. (ML, letter 88, p. 271)

Although they deny every imaginable anthropomorphic God, the adepts acknowledge that there may be a conscious and voluntary or self-determining consciousness of the universe. K.H. writes:

> Did it ever strike you . . . that Universal, like finite, human mind might have two attributes, or a dual power—one the voluntary and conscious, and the other the involuntary and unconscious or the mechanical power? To reconcile the difficulty of many theistic and anti-theistic propositions, both these powers are a philosophical necessity. The possibility of the first or the voluntary and conscious attribute . . . will remain for ever a mere hypothesis, whereas in the finite mind it is a scientific and demonstrated fact. The highest Planetary Spirit is as ignorant of the first as we are, and the hypothesis

will remain one even in Nirvana, as it is a mere inferential possibility, whether there or here. (ML, letter 90, p. 279)

WHY IS THERE EVIL?

In her collected writings, Blavatsky tells us:

> The problem of the origin of evil can be philosophically approached only if the archaic Indian formula is taken as the basis of the argument. Ancient wisdom alone solves the presence of the universal fiend in a satisfactory way. It attributes the birth of Kosmos and the evolution of life to the breaking asunder of primordial, manifested UNITY, into plurality, or the great illusion of form. HOMOGENEITY having transformed itself into Heterogeneity, contrasts have naturally been created: hence sprang what we call EVIL. (CW 8:110)

The eternal ONE has polarized and of necessity that polarization produces the opposites. We can think of nothing that cannot be contrasted with its opposite, or at least with something other than itself. Without that contrast, words would have no meaning. Whatever object or idea that we can imagine has its "other." This is true even of such words as *and* because there is *not and*. We can go on with male-female, mountain-valley, wet-dry, and true-false. Soon we would discover that the examples are endless. The greatest and most difficult of the opposites to understand is that of good and evil. Yet without evil, we could not understand what good is. This simple fact does not sit well with us. It leaves us unsatisfied because we can find no use for evil. Yet evil may have its use. Often people come out of tragedy stronger, more compassionate, even more patient than before. There is an expression in Spanish that sums it up in a few words: "*No hay mal que por bien no venga.*" It translates, "There is no evil from which a good does not come."

St. Augustine was intrigued with the question of evil. Even though he connected it with original sin, he saw that it might have a place in the great scheme of things. In his *Exposition on the Psalms*, he wrote that evil people serve some purpose. He said that every wicked person may be converted, and even if they are not converted, they exist to try and test the righteous. He added that we should not hate evil people because we cannot know if they will persist in their evil ways to the end. Then he issued a warning to the righteous. He said we should not hate evildoers because often when we think we are hating an enemy, we are hating a brother without knowing it.

Annie Besant, second international president of the Theosophical Society, commented that everything grows by struggling against something that opposes. We can easily understand that our muscles would never develop if we did not use them against the force of gravity. Were we to sit stationary in a chair for a month, we would be unable to get up from the chair. We can also see that our mind would not develop were we to spend our entire lives without any mental challenges. It is by using our mind to solve problems that our mind develops. What most of us fail to realize is that the difficult people in our lives provide an opportunity for us to grow psychologically. Unless we can walk away from difficult people, we must develop ways to deal with them. For example, if we are not independently wealthy and we are having a difficult time with our boss, we cannot simply quit the job, especially if jobs are scarce. Perhaps we have been too weak. Perhaps we have allowed the boss to trample on our rights as a fellow worker. The emotional pressure may force us to try to work out the difficulties with the boss. The "evil" of the bad relationship may result in the "good" of making us a stronger, even happier, person.

Many who believe in a personal God are convinced that Satan exists and that he is the source of evil in the world. Others who do not believe in such a spirit yet believe that evil is an independent power in the world. The Masters reject those ideas. They claim that evil, per se, does not exist. It is not an independent power, any more than good is an independent power. Nature is destitute of good or evil, just as electricity is neither good nor bad. It all depends on how human beings use it. It can light our homes or it can be used to torture a victim.

The Masters say that the origin of evil is in "reasoning man." Humanity, not nature, is the source of evil. K.H. asks Sinnett to trace any evil to its source and he will find that it originates in human selfishness and greed. K.H. reasons that evil is the exaggeration of good. He points out that

food, sexual relations, drink, are all natural necessities of life; yet excess in them brings on disease, misery, suffering, mental and physical, and the latter are transmitted as the greatest

evils to future generations, the progeny of the culprits . . .
food, wealth, ambition, and a thousand other things . . .
[become] the source and cause of evil whether in its abundance or through its absence. . . . Therefore it is neither
nature nor an imaginary Deity that has to be blamed, but
human nature made vile by *selfishness*. (ML, letter 88, p. 274)

K.H. then asks Sinnett to think over what he said and he
will have solved a third of the problem of evil.

K.H. next identifies what he calls two thirds of the problem
of evil. What he says has upset many and caused some to reject
everything the adepts teach, but if one suspends judgment and
tries to understand the heart of what is being said, the cold hard
truth of it may become clear. K.H. wrote that two thirds of the
world's evil has been caused by

religion under whatever form and in whatsoever nation. . . .
Ignorance created Gods and cunning took advantage of the
opportunity. Look at India and look at Christendom and
Islam, at Judaism and Fetichism. It is priestly imposture that
rendered these Gods so terrible to man; it is religion that
makes of him the selfish bigot, the fanatic that hates all mankind out of his own sect without rendering him any better or
more moral for it. It is belief in God and Gods that makes
two-thirds of humanity the slaves of a handful of those who
deceive them under the false pretence of saving them. Is not
man ever ready to commit any kind of evil if told that his
God or Gods demand the crime? (ML, letter 88, p. 274)

Since those words were written in the 1880s, mainstream Christianity and no doubt other religions have come a long way. Interfaith cooperation has been growing, and prominent leaders of all religions can be found who denounce intolerance and encourage interreligious cooperation. From Roman Catholic popes to the Dalai Lama, there has been a major effort to encourage respect for all major faiths, and often there are interreligious services. Still among us, of course, are the bigots who denounce all outside of their faith and, from their proud and insular perch, condemn all to hell but themselves.

Although K.H. tells us that one third of the world's evil comes from selfishness and two thirds come from religion, we must not take those fractions literally. In fact, if we look at what K.H. says about the evil caused by religion, we will see that it is also rooted in selfishness and greed, especially as it manifests in a desire for power and a desire to control others. K.H. agrees with the Buddha, who taught: "From ignorance spring all the evils. From knowledge comes the cessation of this mass of misery" (ML, letter 88, p. 275). It is ignorance of our true nature, ignorance of our roots in an eternal ONE that causes us to act selfishly as though we were a law unto ourselves alone.

PHENOMENA VERSUS PHILOSOPHY

Blavatsky came onto the world stage with a staggering amount of occult phenomena. The Masters were never too happy with the display, but they permitted some of it, probably merely to draw people in to learn more of the metaphysical truths in their philosophy.

One of the most amazing displays of Blavatsky's ability to materialize objects happened on a picnic. The first account of it was written by A. P. Sinnett, who published it in the newspaper *The Pioneer* in Allahabad, India, on October 27, 1880. Sinnett wrote that, just before departing for a picnic, he received "a short note" from a Brother. The note informed him that "something would be given" to his wife up on the hill. During lunch, H.P.B. said that the Brother (K.H.) told her to ask the group where they would like to have him leave the note, and that they should select an unlikely place. Sinnett wrote:

After a little talk on the subject, I and my wife selected the inside of her jampan cushion, against which she was then leaning. This is a strong cushion of velvet and worsted work that we have had some years. We were shortly told that the cushion would do. My wife was directed to cut the cushion open. This we found a task of some difficulty as the edges were all very tightly sewn, but a pen-knife conquered them in a little while. . . . When we got the velvet and worsted work cover cut open, we found the inner cushion containing the feathers sewn up in a case of its own. This in turn had to be cut open, and then, buried in the feathers, my wife found a note addressed to me and a brooch—an old familiar brooch which she had had for many years, and which, she tells me, she remembers having picked up off her dressing-table that morning while getting ready to go out, though she afterwards put it down again, and chose another instead.

The note read:

My dear Brother,—This brooch . . . is placed in this very strange place, simply to show to you how very easily a real phenomenon is produced, and how still easier it is to suspect its genuineness. Make of it what you like, even to classing me with confederates.

Morya tried to convince Sinnett that desire to see phenomena was like a drug: craving it did no good. Morya wrote:

Also try to break thro' that great *maya* [illusion] against which occult students, the world over, have always been warned by their teachers—the hankering after phenomena. Like the thirst for drink and opium, it grows with gratification. The Spiritualists are drunken with it. . . . If you cannot be happy without phenomena you will never learn our philosophy. If you want healthy, philosophic thought, and can be satisfied with such—let us correspond. I tell you a profound truth in saying that if you . . . but choose wisdom all other things will be added unto it—in time. It adds no force to our metaphysical truths that our letters are dropped from space on to your lap or come under your pillow. If our philosophy is wrong a *wonder* will not set it right. Put that conviction into your consciousness and let us talk like sensible men. Why should we play with Jack-in-the-box; are not *our* beards grown? . . . The task *is* difficult and K.H. in remembrance of old times, when he loved to quote poetry, asks me to close my letter with the following to your address:

'Does the road wind up-hill all the way?'
'Yes to the very end.'
'Will the day's journey take the whole long day?'
'From morn to night, my friend.'

[From "Up Hill," by Christina Rossetti (1830–1894)]

Knowledge for the mind, like food for the body, is intended to feed and help to growth, but it requires to be well digested and the more thoroughly and slowly the process is carried out the better both for body and mind (ML, letter 42, p. 115).

Chapter 5

KARMA

The word *karma* was used as a technical term only among Asian scholars until A. P. Sinnett published *Esoteric Budhism*, a book he wrote based on what he had learned from the Mahatma Letters. According to the *Oxford English Dictionary*, it was Sinnett's book that introduced the concept of "karma" into popular speech. Frequently when writers mention Sinnett's book they "correct" the spelling of Budhism to "Buddhism." Sinnett's title is correct as he wrote it. The book is not about the religion of Buddhism, esoteric or not. Rather, the title is based on the Sanskrit root *budh*, which translates as "awakened" or "enlightened" (Grimes, *Dictionary of Indian Philosophy*, p. 99). Therefore, his book might have been entitled "Esoteric Enlightenment." Even then it would have been a poor title. Naturally, Sinnett featured the concept of karma in his book, and because the book was widely read by the general public, the word *karma* came into popular language. Today, the word has become part of everyday speech even among those who understand the word to mean "fate."

Many who believe in karma think of it as a law that affects only human affairs. They believe that everything that happens to us is due to our actions in the past. If someone suffers a tragedy, they say it is their bad karma. If they win the lottery, it is their good karma. The adepts have quite a different understanding of karma. To them, karma is the fundamental law of the universe. It is an immutable law, and as such is "eternal and uncreated." The adepts "recognise but one law in the Universe, the law of harmony, of *perfect* EQUILIBRIUM," the law of karma (ML, letter 90, p. 282). An example of this law of perfect equilibrium can be found in homeostasis. When we have a fever, the body fights to restore harmony. When the basic harmony of a system is broken, nature seeks to balance it as water seeks its own level. It is not difficult to see that karma may be nature's law of perfect equilibrium. Yet in Fragment III, verse 300 of *The Voice of the Silence*, H.P.B.'s book on the spiritual life, we read that "Compassion is no attribute. It is the Law of laws—eternal Harmony."

Is it possible that karma and compassion are one and the same law? The question is not easy to answer. All we can say is that perfect equilibrium may only be obtained in the state called "*pralaya*" in Indian and Theosophical philosophy, and "maximum entropy" in scientific terms. Primordial unity, or perfect equilibrium, is rent asunder when our universe appears out of the void. Thereafter, karma works to restore that unity, moving us once again to maximum entropy. Compassion for all living beings also works to restore harmony. Perhaps the two are but different aspects of the same law.

Karma is a Sanskrit word that means "action." The theory of karma states that for every action there is a reaction. This is said to be true not only for physical actions, but for emotional, mental, and spiritual actions. As *The Voice of the Silence* (Fragment II, verses 147–148) puts it:

> E'en wasted smoke remains not traceless. "A harsh word uttered in past lives, is not destroyed but ever comes again." The pepper plant will not give birth to roses, nor the sweet jessamine's silver star to thorn or thistle turn. Thou canst create this day thy chances for thy morrow. In the Great Journey, causes sown each hour bear each its harvest of effects, for rigid Justice rules the World. With mighty sweep of never-erring action, it brings to mortals lives of weal or woe, the Karmic progeny of all our former thoughts and deeds.

The karma we create by thought, word, and deed determines our birth, our parents, our country, our physical and psychological condition, and certain events and meetings in our next life. As K.H. says, "*Karma* is your *only* personality to be when you step beyond" (ML, letter 47, p. 131). But the law of karma is true not only for human action but for *every* action throughout the universe. It is the law of laws. If that is so, then no one can say that they know the consequences of every action at every level. Yet we often hear people saying such things as "You have cancer because you felt resentful." How do they know? There are so many variables involved in most actions that it would take omniscience to predict the results in every case.

A simple example may help us understand how variables affect karmic results. Let us say that we have a professional ballplayer facing a plate-glass window at about twenty-five yards. He throws a ball as hard as he can. It reaches a speed of seventy-five miles per hour. What would happen to the plate-glass window? Clearly it would break. But can we say that is inevitable? What if another professional ballplayer were standing in front of that window holding a catcher's mitt and he reached up and caught the ball? That variable would prevent the window from being broken. Consider how many variables there must be at the subjective level of action. We might feel intense anger at someone. Can we accurately predict the consequences of that action? If the recipient of the anger is an angry person, a physical fight might ensue. If that person is a peaceful, compassionate person, however, he might respond with inner calm and a soft voice and neutralize the anger rather than increase it. That calm response could easily calm us, thus reducing the effects of our anger. The principle of inertia provides a good example of karma. A body at rest tends to remain at rest unless acted upon by an outside force, and a body in motion tends to remain in motion unless acted upon by an outside force. The number of "outside forces" at the subjective level is surely many times more than those at a merely physical level.

A common popular view of karma is that nearly everything that happens to us in this life is the result of something we did in a past life. If we take a hard look at the pleasant and unpleasant things that happen to us in our lives, it will almost certainly become clear that most of what happens to us can be traced back to our actions in this life. In one sense we do not get our karma from the past. We *are* our karma from the past. The way we live in this life gives us an opportunity to change our future.

Many who accept the concept of karma believe that there are no accidents and that whatever happens to us is the result of our personal past karma. They seem to think that if a plane carrying three hundred people crashes and all are killed, it is the karma of every single passenger on that plane. The plane crash *was* due to karma, but that karma may have been simply the fact that the engines failed, or there was an explosion or fire on the plane. It is highly unlikely that it was the karma of all three hundred passengers to die in the crash. It may have been that it was not the personal karma of any of them to die in the crash. K.H. makes this possibility clear when he writes: "Accidents occur under the most various circumstances; and men are not only killed *accidentally*, or die as *suicides* but are also *murdered*" (ML, letter 76, p. 239). Each of us may have an appointed time to die, but if an accident takes our life before our "due date," K.H. claims that "accidents . . . will always find their reward in a future life" (ML, letter 88, p. 274).

We create our own individual karma through personal relationships. Little or no karma is created by our meetings with store clerks or other individuals we encounter in a casual way. Our relationships with family members, friends, and lovers are quite a different matter. It is through personal love and hate that we bind ourselves to others and to the fruits of our actions with them. Says K.H.: "*Love* and *Hatred* are the only *immortal* feelings" (ML, letter 70C, p. 209). If that is so, then if we wish to avoid entanglement with the difficult people we meet in life, we had better refrain from hating them. It may be we can never love them, but we can maintain a neutral attitude toward them, neither loving nor hating them but accepting them as fellow human beings with their own problems with which we do not want to be involved.

Individual karma can accrue and carry over into future lives. The Masters claim they have learned how to avoid making individual karma. The Masters have exhausted their *personal* karma. Since individual karma is acquired through personal relationships, the Masters do not enter into personal relationships and therefore remain single and celibate. They are not free of personal preferences and say that they enjoy the company of some people more than others, but that is far different from being involved in personal relationships. The Masters will work with an individual only when they believe that individual can be helpful in their work for humanity. That is an impersonal, cooperative venture rather than a personal relationship.

Although the Masters are free of personal karma, they are not free of universal karma. Should a war approach their peaceful precincts, they would have to act to protect themselves. For example, they might set up an illusory scene of an impassible canyon, thus stopping the advancing army from approaching them. That is karma in action, but it is not personal karma. Personal karma is understood to be personal action that brings personal consequences. It is the kind of action that can be "stored up" for release in this or future incarnations.

A key to understanding how not to create more personal karma lies in motive. Writing to Sinnett, K.H. said, "our respective standards of right and wrong will never agree together, since *motive* is everything for us, and . . . you will never go beyond appearances" (ML, letter 92, p. 295). If we act out of personal motives, then inevitably the consequences of our actions eventually come back to us personally. If, however, the inner self acts *through* us, then the consequences come back to the inner self. The Masters say that they "show no favors." While they are friendly to many, they claim not to become entangled in personal relationships of a binding nature. They know that such relationships create personal karma that would require them to remain on the "wheel of birth."

In addition to individual karma, groups, institutions, and nations have their collective karma. As in the example of a plane crash that kills hundreds of people, it is not likely that everyone who dies in a war dies because of karma they have *personally* created in the past. Individuals may and do protest the actions of their governments at times, but whatever their government does will most likely affect them. The nation creates its own karma, and citizens of that nation are bound to be part of the national karma. In a letter to C. W. Leadbeater, K.H. wrote, "There is also the collective karma of *the caste you belong to* to be considered." K.H. wrote that because Leadbeater was a priest of the Anglican Church, and Christian missionaries at the time would "stop before nothing to ruin the reputation of the Founders" of the Theosophical Society (LMW1:28).

Once we realize that karma is the fundamental law of the universe, we should be humble enough to accept the fact that we would have to be omniscient to be able to predict the karmic consequences of every action, especially those actions created by our interpersonal relationships.

Chapter 6

OUR SEVENFOLD NATURE

When Blavatsky wrote *Isis Unveiled*, she said that we human beings have a threefold nature. Using St. Paul's terms, she called them "spirit," "soul," and "body." Then when she wrote *The Secret Doctrine*, she said that we have seven major aspects that she called "principles." Furthermore, in that same work, she claimed that two of these, the body and what she called "atma," were not principles at all. Confounding the issue, she added that there was really only one principle, not seven.

The apparent confusion can be cleared up if we remember that the cornerstone of Theosophical philosophy is fundamental unity. Theosophy postulates that everything in the universe, from galaxies to grains of sand and from angels to insects, is rooted in one, ultimately indivisible reality. Each creature and each thing, including every human being, is but a transient state within that reality, very much as waves are transient states within the sea. The waves have a distinct existence, but one cannot take the wave out of the sea and say: "Here is the wave, and there is the sea." These two are one. Similarly, everyone knows that H_2O can appear as steam, water, or ice. By using the analogy of H_2O, we can see that, just as steam, water, and ice are states of one substance, our seven principles may be states of one reality. Therefore, every aspect of our nature can be understood to be a different state of one substance. There are seven, yet there is only one. It is from this principle of fundamental unity that the Theosophical Society derives its first objective, that of forming a nucleus of the universal brotherhood of humanity. (Note that the Theosophical Society referred to objectives as "objects.") That nucleus consists of those who have to some extent realized their ultimate unity with all others and all else, and who attempt to live accordingly.

Everyone can identify several of the seven human principles within themselves. No matter what our philosophy, we all know that we are conscious, and we have a body, emotions, and a mind. Everyone agrees about that, even if some say that consciousness, emotions, and mind are simply by-products of chemical actions in the brain. In addition to the four agreed-upon principles, many believe that we have a spiritual nature. The definitions of *spiritual* vary, however, and most definitions are so vague that they leave us uncertain as to whether or not we have an identifiable spiritual nature.

According to Theosophy, three of our principles are directly associated with the spiritual nature. Taken together, those three principles are known variously as our "inner self," the "reincarnating ego," or the "higher self." Although the inner self may be thought of as consisting of three principles, we experience them as one. Each of our seven principles has a Sanskrit name used in Theosophical discussions. Usually, the reason for this is because there are no English equivalent terms.

The first of the three principles that constitute the inner self is called "atma." It is said to be our root in the Eternal and our only truly immortal self. To get some sense of this in ourselves, it might be helpful to ponder a summary of what H.P.B. called the first fundamental proposition of her *Secret Doctrine*:

An Omnipresent, Eternal, Boundless, and Immutable PRINCIPLE on which all speculation is impossible, since it transcends the power of human conception and could only be dwarfed by any human expression or similitude. It is beyond the range and reach of thought—in the words of the *Mandukya Upanishad*, "unthinkable and unspeakable." (SD 1:14)

While that principle is "unthinkable and unspeakable," we can get some sense of it if we think of eternal, boundless space. Space is the one constant that is always present. Space is there whether or not there is anything or anyone occupying it. It was there before the big bang that began the universe, and as far as we can imagine, it will be there when the universe disintegrates. Now, if we consider the possibility that space is eternal, undifferentiated consciousness, we may come close to understanding what atma is.

Atma or atman is the universal spirit, sometimes called "the divine monad." It is our root in the Eternal. Each of us is a point in that universal reality, which is best thought of as unconditioned consciousness, consciousness without an object. For us it is nearly impossible to imagine consciousness without an object, so we ask: "Conscious of what?" But in unconditioned consciousness, there is no "what." If you will recall a time when you just awoke from sleep, you will almost certainly remember that, for a nanosecond, there was only a sense of "am," a sense of what H.P.B. called "beness." It was neither joyful nor sorrowful. It was without any identifiable thought or feeling. It was simply, "I am," and even the "I" was absent.

When we experience a state of consciousness, objects of consciousness come into our minds. "Where am I?" we might ask, or "What is today and what must I do today?" Depending on the answers to those questions, we begin to experience thought and emotion. If it is a day we are going on vacation, we would most likely feel happy. If it is a day for major surgery, we would probably feel anxious or fearful. The objects of consciousness affect our thought and our emotions, but consciousness alone simply is. That consciousness is said to be "the ground of our being." It is not only our ground as a human being, but also the ground of being in all creatures. Theosophical philosophy teaches that there is no such thing as matter without consciousness or consciousness without matter. Therefore, from a Theosophical perspective, even rocks are conscious. We have no hard evidence for this teaching, but the fact that everything is self-moving suggests the possibility that in some dim sense everything is "alive" and therefore conscious. Of course rocks do not move from place to place, but their atomic structure is in constant motion.

As a point, atma has no dimensions whatsoever. It has one characteristic only, that of location. It cannot be in two places at the same time. Consider the fact that when you are on the phone and someone in the room speaks to you, you can hear both individuals but you cannot *listen* to both at the same time. Most likely you will ask the person on the phone to hold on a moment and then ask the person in the room to say what they wish to say to you. You are one-pointed in consciousness. Consider also that in observing an optical illusion, you can focus on only one of the two images at a time. You may know that part of one image is another part of the other, but you can only focus on one at a time. You are one-pointed in consciousness.

If you attempt to imagine yourself on two sides of a street at the same time, you may see two of you from above the street, at street level, or see one from one side of the street and then from the other. In all cases, however, your true self is at a third point observing two images of yourself at a distance. You are one-pointed in consciousness.

Your consciousness can be centered in any one of our other six principles. We can be acutely aware of our big toe, especially if we have just stubbed it. We can be centered in our emotions so thoroughly that it is possible in traumatic situations, such as being shot, that we may be unaware of the physical damage until sometime after the impact. It is also possible to be so centered in our mind when we are working or studying that we are totally unaware of our hunger until we take a break and notice hunger pangs. We are one-pointed in consciousness.

The second principle of the inner self is called "buddhi." That word comes from a Sanskrit root *budh* meaning "awake." Metaphorically, the Buddha is the one who is awake whereas others are asleep. Every human being may eventually awaken in the experience called "enlightenment." There is a line in the New Testament attributed to Jesus that parallels this idea. He said, "Let the dead bury their dead." The metaphor is different but it may well have the same meaning.

Buddhi is the universal soul or mind, sometimes called the "oversoul." It has been described as our spiritual soul, cosmic ideation, intuition (not as a psychic hunch but as insight), wisdom, and bliss. It is that state of consciousness from which we get flashes of understanding. All our thoughts surrounding an issue suddenly come together in the "ah-ha" experience. It is buddhi that integrates them all and flashes a truth into our minds. Buddhi may be thought of as ultimate Truth. If so, what does buddhi have to do with bliss?

It should take only a moment's reflection to realize that whenever we suddenly understand a principle, we feel joyful. We are even likely to feel more energetic. In that split second when we experience a flash of understanding, there is no "me." For far less than a second, there is only that truth and a joyous and peaceful response to it that seems to radiate through us. In the moment of understanding, there is no awareness of the "me" or even of time. There is only the truth itself. The knower and the known have become one. This is far different from being informed of a fact. Should we be told about a dreadful tragedy, we may do whatever we can to be of help, but the news of the tragedy does not make us feel happy. True, when we learn some facts, they make us happy; but that happiness does not feel the same as the joy and peace we experience when we understand a principle. One can think of many examples such as suddenly understanding a mathematical principle. Einstein testified to this when he said that when he understood that $E = mc^2$, it was akin to a mystical experience.

Someone once said that consciousness is the singular of which there is no plural. According to Theosophical teachings, each of us is a point in universal consciousness. Taken together, atma and buddhi are the spirit. They are universal, not individual. If buddhi is thought of as cosmic ideation, even as truth itself, then surely it is not individual. There cannot be a different truth for different people. If there were, then truth would have no meaning. The truth is always there, whether we are aware of it or not.

In a letter to Hume and Sinnett, K.H. made what may appear to be a curious statement about atma and buddhi. He wrote that "neither Atma nor Buddhi ever were *within* man." He added that Plato and Pythagoras taught that

the *demonium* or this *nous* [atma and buddhi] always remained without the body; that it floated and overshadowed, so to say, the extreme part of man's head, it is only the vulgar who think it is within them. . . . The permanent never merges with the impermanent although the two are one. But it is only when all outward appearances are gone that there is left that one principle of life which exists independently of all external phenomena. It is the fire that burns in the eternal light, when the fuel is expended and the flame is extinguished; for that fire is neither in the flame nor in the fuel, nor yet inside either of the two but above beneath and everywhere. (ML, letter 72, p. 217)

Our understanding of a truth happens when for a moment our mind is in harmony with that realm of truth beyond the physical brain. We might say that flash of understanding comes when our mind is isomorphic with the divine mind. Our mind is an aspect of the inner self. It is our enduring individuality, the reincarnating ego, the human soul. The Sanskrit word for it is *manas*, usually translated as *mind*. But when we think of "mind," we usually understand "intellect." Manas is much more than intellect. One may have little intellectual ability and yet be a great artist, or be one who has the ability to understand and work well with people. According to H.P.B., manas is our unique individuality. Manas is our human soul. Yet manas appears to be dual while we are incarnate. That is because manas can be focused on the abstract, on principles, or it can be focused on the sensate world filled with emotion and desire. When our mind is focused on the abstract, on principles, on a truth, it is united to buddhi and is called "buddhi-manas." Buddhi-manas has been called "the higher mind" because it is the ability we possess to comprehend the abstract. It is our ability to conceptualize and to understand principles. We and animals can see many different types of chairs, but unlike most if not all animals, only humans can form the concept of "chairness." Concepts are abstract. We see chairs, but no one will ever see "chairness." The ability to form concepts is what differentiates us from the rest. It is buddhi-manas that gives us that ability. Buddhi-manas is our spiritual soul, our higher mind, our individuality, our reincarnating self.

The Masters claim that the human race has been rapidly developing the powers of the mind for centuries. Whether or not one believes in Masters, it is obvious that humanity has been developing mental ability for many years. It is now common in our culture to regard the intellect as the supreme human power. K.H. would not agree with that assessment. Referring to a mystery that baffled Sinnett, K.H. wrote:

If, throwing aside every preconceived idea, you could TRY and impress yourself with this profound truth that intellect is not all powerful by itself; that to become "a mover of mountains" it has first to receive life and light from its higher principle—Spirit [atma-buddhi] . . . you would soon read the mystery right. (ML, letter 126, p. 426)

From the point of view of the Masters, one

may be a Bacon or an Aristotle in knowledge, and still not even make his current felt a feather's weight by [the Masters], if his power is confined to the *Manas*. The supreme energy resides in the *Buddhi*; latent—when wedded to *Atman* alone, active and irresistible when galvanized by the *essence* of "Manas" and when none of the dross of the latter commingles with that pure essence to weigh it down by its finite nature. *Manas*, pure and simple, is of a lower degree, and of the earth earthly: and so your greatest men count but as nonentities in the arena where greatness is measured by the standard of spiritual development. (ML, letter 111, p. 375)

If we take but a moment to reflect on it, we will realize that when we are struggling to understand something, the understanding we need is latent. It is mere potential, and so far as we are concerned, while we are struggling, it is nonexistent. Only when understanding flashes on our mind does it become active and irresistible.

Another curious link between buddhi and manas is cited by K.H. in a letter to Francesca Arundale, in which he says:

Good resolutions are mind-painted pictures of good *deeds*: fancies, day-dreams, whisperings of the *Buddhi* to the *Manas*. If we encourage them they will not fade away like a dissolving mirage in the Shamo [that is, Gobi] desert, but grow stronger and stronger until one's whole life becomes the expression and outward proof of the divine motive within. (LMW1:52)

The second aspect of manas is one we share with animals. It is the ability to perceive the outer world and its objects in our mind. That aspect is our analytical mind, the mind that can distinguish one thing from another. This aspect of manas has been called "the lower mind," but that phrase tends to make us think it is a "bad" mind whereas the higher mind is a "good" mind. In fact, the higher and lower minds are simply aspects of one mind and neither is good nor bad, any more than one kidney is good and the other is bad. The early Theosophical literature called that second aspect of our mind "kama-manas," *kama* being essentially our emotional nature. The phrase "kama-manas" is a good one because if you observe your mind you will probably discover that you cannot have a thought without some emotion associated with it, and you cannot have emotion without some thought associated with it. We know the difference between a thought and an emotion, but the two always come together like two sides of one coin. Joy Mills, a past president of the Theosophical Society in America and international lecturer on Theosophy, has made up a word for the combination of emotion and thought. She calls it "flinking." Kama-manas is where the average person is centered. It is the feeling-thinking process we call "me." Rare is the person who can willfully center consciousness in buddhi-manas. The one who can do that at will and operate from that state of consciousness is an adept.

Another feature of kama-manas is one with which we are all familiar. It is the associative principle of the mind. It is the ability to associate one thought or one perception with another, an ability we share with animals. The famous experiment of Pavlov illustrates this beautifully. A bell is rung and the dog is fed. This is repeated a number of times, and then the bell is rung but the dog is not fed. Yet, the dog salivates on hearing the bell because he has associated the bell with food. The advertising industry uses this ability to their advantage. They associate their product with prestige, success, finding a lover, and more. Advertisements suggest that you are nobody if you don't have their product. What they hope is that when you see their product you will unconsciously or even consciously associate it with your desire and purchase the product. Word association tests also reveal this ability and can be used to detect normal versus abnormal psychological states. The average person might respond *fork* to the word *knife*, but a disturbed person might associate *murder* with that word.

Some have likened the mind to a thief, but since buddhi-manas is the higher self, it could not be a thief. Geoffrey Hodson, a prominent Theosophist of the last century, suggested that the two thieves crucified next to Christ may represent buddhi-manas and kama-manas. The thief on the right of Jesus asked him to remember him when he came into his kingly power, and Jesus responded, "Truly, I say to you, today you will be with me in Paradise." Buddhi-manas is an aspect of the inner self and therefore survives bodily death. The other thief represents kama-manas, that aspect of mind that is incapable of union with the Eternal. That "thief" wants to save his personal ego, but as Jesus pointed out in another passage: "For whosoever will save his life shall lose it: and whosoever will lose his life for my sake shall find it." If we identify with kama-manas and our body, then we shall surely lose our life.

In Fragment I of *The Voice of the Silence*, we find a reference to mind that has perplexed many. It is the statement, "The Mind is the great Slayer of the Real. Let the Disciple slay the Slayer."

The "Slayer" is kama-manas, but not the principles of kama and manas. Rather it is the illusion that we *are* kama-manas and that there is nothing more to us than it and our body. It is the feeling-thinking nature with which we have so thoroughly identified and which we call "me." The self-image of *me* is built up from childhood. We quickly learn whether we are male or female. Then we learn how our culture expects boys to behave and how it expects girls to behave. Some people are comfortable with that behavior and some are not. We get a sense of our own self-worth, or lack of it, by the way we are treated by parents, society, and our peers. Our self-image is formed from all of that and more. If when young we try to express ourselves in public and we are ridiculed or laughed at, we may decide not ever to speak in public again. With that mortifying experience burned on our brain, at age fifty we may say, "I am a shy person." We are living in past experience and calling it "me." It is this feeling-thinking false self (kama-manas) that is the slayer of the real, and it is that false self-image that must be slain.

The principle of kama, already mentioned above, is not part of our inner self. Rather, it is an important aspect of our personality. *Kama* is often translated as *desire* or *craving*, and, although that is its chief characteristic, kama is our emotional nature in its totality. Spiritual literature often advises us to kill our desire, but if we had no desire we would do nothing. Kama is not bad. It is a universal principle localized in us. From one point of view, even plants have "desire." They crave water and sunlight, perhaps not in the conscious way that we crave something, but nonetheless they are driven to obtain what they need. It is not kama itself that is the problem. It is identification with kama and our attachments to the objects of desire that are the problem, and that is what must be slain.

We might say that each of us is an individual, localized field of kama and manas, but the next principle, though experienced locally, is itself a universal in the same way that atma and buddhi are universals. That principle is called "*prana*." It is our vital energy. It is the energy of life itself, and it pulses through everything. Blavatsky calls *prana* "the Universal Life" and says that life is "in reality, Divinity, Parabrahman, the Universal Deity" (CW 12:704, 707). There are people who seem to exhibit strong vital energy throughout their lives, and there are others who seem to have very little of it. One day we may feel full of energy and another day feel exhausted. *Prana* flows through us, but it is not a localized field or a body. It is this vital energy, or *prana*, that spiritual healers allegedly use to heal their clients.

Prana flows through our next principle, that of the *linga sharira*, or what some secondary Theosophical literature has called the "etheric double." As with all our principles, we can regard this one as a "field," a word that Blavatsky would almost certainly have used to describe it had she known about fields. H.P.B. claimed that this principle is formed in the womb before the physical body is formed. In her Esoteric Section Instructions, she writes, "It is first in the womb and then comes the germ that fructifies it, from the male parent" (CW 12:704). That rather amazing statement implies that we begin the incarnation process even before conception. The *linga sharira* forms the physical body much in the same way as the field of a bar magnet molds iron filings in its presence. This field is not a static field, however. It is a dynamic, ever-changing field. One remarkable piece of evidence to support this theory is that, as a chicken is developing within the egg, there begins to be a pulse at the exact spot where the heart *will be* formed. There is as yet no heart there, but the pulsing is there. Theoretically, the pulsing is evidence for a dynamic force field that is molding the physical heart.

Blavatsky tells us that the *linga sharira* "serves as the intermediary between *prana* and [the body]" (CW 12:704, 705). Some gifted clairvoyants report seeing this intermediary link lift out of the body during anesthesia. During general anesthesia, the *linga sharira* seems to "float" above the body. During local anesthesia, say of the hand, only that portion of the *linga sharira* may be seen to leave the physical hand. Apparently with the link out of the body, no pain can be felt. This does not deny what anesthesiologists say about the effects of the drug, but it does offer a further explanation of why we feel no pain during anesthesia. When the *linga sharira* sinks back into the body, we usually need painkiller medication.

Lastly we come to the physical body, with which we are all familiar. Our body is said to be the "*upadhi*" (vehicle) of every principle. Each one of our principles is expressed through the physical body and each affects the body in some way. It has been demonstrated that at least some individuals can lower their blood pressure or slow their heart rate by using the mind (manas). We know that when emotionally excited, the body releases adrenaline, and our mental state can affect our body positively or negatively.

By recalling the fact that we can focus our consciousness in any one of our principles, and remembering that atma (consciousness itself) may be considered the divine ground of being, it is not difficult to understand St. Paul's statement, "Know ye not that ye are the temple of God, and that the Spirit of God dwelleth in you?"

Chapter 7

FROM DEATH
TO REBIRTH

I s it possible that we survive bodily death? That question has intrigued men and women ever since Adam and Eve left the mythological Garden of Eden. Theories on the subject range from that of total extinction to eternal life in some sort of heaven or hell.

The near-death experiences (NDEs) have given us some evidence that consciousness may exist outside our bodies. Yet, a great deal of what has been reported by those who have been resuscitated from clinical death (a state lacking any vital signs) can be explained by what is presumed to happen to the brain at death. Frequent reports of light, a life review, of going through a tunnel, meeting those who have died, and even the sensation of being out of body are among the experiences that some say are all due to drugs and what is happening to the brain as it dies. While a reasonable person must consider the possibility that those experiences are all hallucinatory, there is one commonly reported

NDE that seems to be impossible to explain by any purely physical means. It is that of reports that the dying individual exited the body and traveled to another place, saw what was there, and returned to report a scene that was later verified by another person.

One such case involves a woman who was rushed to a hospital in the middle of the night. She "died" in the hospital and was resuscitated. At a visit from her social worker, the woman reported that while out of the body, she had traveled to an upper floor of the hospital and saw a blue sneaker on a windowsill. She asked her social worker to go to that window and look for the sneaker. Fortunately, the social worker did as asked, and she discovered the blue sneaker exactly where the patient had described it. Having arrived at the hospital in the middle of the night with no possibility of seeing a blue sneaker on a windowsill of an upper floor of the hospital, it would seem the only reasonable explanation is that the patient did indeed leave the body and see that sneaker. Kenneth Ring, professor emeritus of psychology at the University of Connecticut and a researcher within the field of near-death studies, has documented and verified numerous other cases of out-of-body experiences.

Often, those who have been resuscitated say that there is what we might call a "line-pass-not" that is seen as a chasm, or in Carl Jung's case when he saw his deceased wife, a stage. Those individuals seem to know that if they cross that line, they will be unable to return to the body. They will be truly dead. Kenneth Ring has received thousands of responses to questionnaires he sent to people who have had a near-death experience, and he jokingly says that it is hard to get the questionnaires back from those who have crossed the line. The reports that do come back provide strong evidence that we can be conscious outside of our body, but that evidence cannot be extended to saying that we survive after crossing the line. Yet, it seems reasonable to assume that we do, especially when we have other supportive evidence for survival of bodily death.

Perhaps the most commonly reported near-death experience is that of having a complete life review when vital signs cease. It is only in relatively recent years that we have many documented cases of this phenomenon, but there have been reports of it long before modern medicine was able to resuscitate people. The Masters claim that this is something that happens to all of us at death. K.H. wrote:

No man dies insane or unconscious—as some physiologists assert. Even a *madman*, or one in a fit of *delirium tremens* will have his instant of perfect lucidity at the moment of death, though unable to say so to those present. The man may often appear dead. Yet from the last pulsation, from and between the last throbbing of his heart and the moment when the last spark of animal heat leaves the body—the *brain thinks* and the *Ego* lives over in those few brief seconds his whole life over again. (ML, letter 93B, p. 326)

We not only relive our whole life in those few seconds, most of us will continue to identify with the life just lived for quite some time after death.

H.P.B. (*Key*, p. 162) tells us:

> For one short instant the *personal* becomes one with the *individual* and all-knowing *Ego*. But this instant is enough to show to him the whole chain of causes which have been at work during his life. He sees and now understands himself as he is, unadorned by flattery or self-deception. He reads his life, remaining as a spectator looking down into the arena he is quitting; he feels and knows the justice of all the suffering that has overtaken him.

In some cases the inner self recalls something that the dying brain could not have known. H.P.B. gives the following example of a man who was resuscitated after losing consciousness:

> the patient slightly lifted his head and began talking rapidly in Flemish, a language no one around him, nor yet himself, understood. Offered a pencil and a piece of white cardboard, he wrote with great rapidity several lines in that language— very correctly, as was ascertained later on—fell back, and died. When translated—the writing was found to refer to a very prosaic affair. He had suddenly recollected, he wrote, that he owed a certain man a sum of fifteen francs since 1868—hence more than twenty years—and desired it to be paid. But why write his last wish in Flemish? The defunct was a native of Antwerp, but had left his country in childhood, without ever knowing the language, and having passed all his life in Paris, could speak and write only in French.

Evidently [the memory] did not emanate from his *physical* brain alone, but rather from his spiritual memory, that of the *Higher Ego* (Manas or the re-incarnating individuality). The fact of his speaking and writing Flemish, a language that he had heard at a time of life when he could not yet speak himself, is an additional proof. *The* EGO is *almost omniscient in its immortal nature.* (CW 11:448)

Blavatsky (*Key*, pp. 162–163) assures us:

As the man at the moment of death has a / retrospective insight into the life he has led, so, at the moment he is reborn on to earth, the *Ego*, awaking from the state of Devachan, has a prospective vision of the life which awaits him, and realizes all the causes that have led to it. He realizes them and sees futurity, because it is between Devachan and re-birth that the *Ego* regains his full *manasic* consciousness, and rebecomes for a short time the god he was, before, in compliance with Karmic law, he first descended into matter and incarnated in the first man of flesh. The "golden thread" sees all its "pearls" and misses not one of them.

There is a similarity between sleep and death, but also a great difference. In sleep the inner self is connected to the personality by what we might call a "magnetic link." At death that link is broken. A possible reference to this phenomenon may be found in Ecclesiastes 12:6–7:

Or ever the silver cord be loosed, or the golden bowl be broken, or the pitcher be broken at the fountain, or the wheel broken at the cistern, and the dust returns to the earth as it was and the spirit returns to God who gave it.

In sleep we may have what amounts to objective experiences, but they will not be remembered unless the memory of them is impressed on the brain on awakening. One example of this is that of a man who dreamed he was communicating with a friend while out of body during sleep. The dream was intensely vivid, so when the man met his friend the next day he asked, "Did you dream about me last night?" The answer was a surprised "Yes," and when told the particulars of the dream, the friend acknowledged that he had had the same dream. In all likelihood the "dream" was no dream at all, but an objective, albeit out-of-body, experience.

Immediately after death it is possible for the dead to appear to someone they love. Such apparitions of the newly dead have been widely reported by many people. The ability to do this does not last for long because soon after the moment of death we drift into unconsciousness and enter that state called the "gestation period." According to some clairvoyants, the aura is reorganized during this period and because of that a gifted clairvoyant can tell the difference between someone who is out of body during sleep and one who is dead.

At death the lower principles are cut off from the true self and become a shell. That shell is our animal nature, and it is the shells that are animated by mediums who claim they have contacted the departed and produced them through a séance. The shells have a life of their own and survive for a while, but eventually they disintegrate. Just as the atoms of our body may become part of a plant, animal, or eventually even another person, so do the atoms of the psychological shell go back to the common pool. If the defunct individual has led a coarse emotional life full of the lower emotions such as anger and lust, the atoms of his lower self may become part of an animal. This is the grain of truth in the doctrine of transmigration. The reincarnating Ego does not become an animal, but the cast-off mental and emotional remains may become part of an animal's nature. The inner self, the true self, cannot go backward. Instead, it soon enters a state of consciousness that the Masters call "devachan," a state of intense happiness wherein we live out our highest spiritual ideals. Although it is an illusion, we are convinced that all our friends and loved ones are with us. We no longer suffer any kind of pain, and even the memory of pain is gone. Our experience in devachan exists entirely in our own mind, but it is every bit as real to us as our physical experience is real to us when we are alive.

In her *Key to Theosophy* (p. 138), Blavatsky explains that "crimes and sins committed on a plane of objectivity and in a world of matter, cannot receive punishment in a world of pure subjectivity," and she adds, "We believe in no hell or paradise as localities; in no objective hell-fires and worms that never die, nor in any Jerusalems with streets paved with sapphires and diamonds. What we believe in is a *post-mortem state* or mental condition, such as we are in during a vivid dream."

There are two distinct stages of experience in devachan. The first is called the "*rupa*" (form) stage. It is in that state of consciousness that we live out all of the spiritual aspirations that we had during earth life. As those ideals are being exhausted, the personal self begins to fade away and finally "dies." That death, however, has little resemblance to the physical death that is often preceded by pain and fear. It is more like going to sleep. When that "second death" occurs, our inner self enters the final stage of devachan, the *arupa* (formless) stage. It is there that we live in a state of spiritual bliss from a few to a few thousand years depending on the karma we have created during our stay in the world of causes, the physical world.

While the vast majority of people have their reward in devachan, the convinced materialist does not, but the lack of reward must not be considered a punishment or suffering of any kind. In Section 9 of *The Key to Theosophy* (p. 157), Blavatsky tells us, "If [the scientific materialists] say that self-consciousness ceases with the body, then in their case they simply utter an unconscious prophecy, for once they are firmly convinced of what they assert, no conscious after-life is possible for them." They simply remain unconscious until they awaken in their next incarnation.

The physical world is the world of causes. Between incarnations we cannot develop a talent that we had not begun to develop while still living. We can, however, further develop a talent already begun. For example, a musical or artistic talent can be further developed in devachan because devachan is "an idealized and subjective continuation of earth-life." Blavatsky assures us:

Immense growths, for example, of knowledge itself are possible in Devachan, for the spiritual entity which has begun the "pursuit" of such knowledge during life. Nothing can happen to a spirit in Devachan, the keynote of which has not been struck during life; the conditions of a subjective existence are such that the importation of quite external impulses and alien thoughts is impossible. But the seed of thought once sown, the current of thoughts once set going . . . and then its developments in Devachan may be infinite. (CW 4:444–445)

The karmic consequences of our misdeeds, our "sins" will not affect us in the after-death state. H.P.B. tells us that they "remain as *Karmic effects*, as germs, hanging in the atmosphere of the terrestrial plane, ready to come to life, as so many avenging fiends, to attach themselves to the new personality of the Ego when it reincarnates" (*Key*, p. 154). "Our philosophy teaches that Karmic punishment reaches the Ego only in its next incarnation. After death it receives only the reward for the unmerited sufferings endured during its past incarnation" (*Key*, p. 161). This theory may not seem unreasonable if we think of the karmic "germs" as being somehow magnetically connected to the inner self. They may be likened to static electricity that, once built up in us, is latent until conditions are right for it to be released as a shock. The karma of our misdeeds may be thought of in a similar way. The right conditions are to be found only during incarnation. Between incarnations those germs are latent.

When the Masters wrote their letters to A. P. Sinnett, Spiritualism was extremely popular in Europe and in the United States. Many believed that they could communicate with the dead through mediums. The Masters wanted to make it clear that in almost all cases it was impossible to contact the dead directly and that the attempt to do so was harmful to the health of those making the attempt. In fact, they said that the process was "disintegrative" to the medium. Yet, in spite of their strong language condemning mediumship, the adepts leave an opening to *indirect* communication with the dead. K.H. told Sinnett that he was mistaken in his belief "that 'the spirits of the departed hold *direct* psychic communication with Souls that are still connected with a human body'—for, they do not" (ML, letter 18, p. 63). If there were no possible communication between the two, why would K.H. have emphasized the word *direct*? Surely he was implying that there could be *indirect* communication, perhaps in dreams, perhaps in sensing the presence of a loved one who had died. What the adept was emphatically denying was the apparition of the departed in a séance room.

The Masters teach that love is immortal and that it can reach those in devachan, and those still living can be affected by the love coming from one in devachan. For reasons mentioned above, however, the devachanee will be totally unaware of any psychological or physical suffering of those still living. Surely we can say that love between the living and those in devachan is a form of indirect communication.

In her *Key to Theosophy* (p. 150), Blavatsky says of the following after death:

We are with those whom we have lost in material form, and far, far nearer to them now, than when they were alive. And it is not only in the fancy of the *Devachanee*, as some may imagine, but in reality. For pure divine love is not merely the blossom of a human heart, but has its roots in eternity. Spiritual holy love is immortal, and Karma brings sooner or later all those who loved each other with such a spiritual affection to incarnate once more in the same family group. Again we say that love beyond the grave, illusion though you may call it, has a magic and divine potency which reacts on the living. A mother's *Ego* filled with love for the imaginary children it sees near itself, living a life of happiness, as real to *it* as when on earth—that love will always be felt by the children in flesh. It will manifest in their dreams, and often in various events . . . for love is a strong shield, and is not limited by space or time.

K.H. tells us that we lapse into unconsciousness at death for a few hours to a few months, and all memory is annihilated. He says that memory (and therefore consciousness) returns to the reincarnating ego "slowly and gradually toward the end of the gestation [period] . . . the Ego does not fall headlong but sinks into it gradually and by easy stages" (ML, letter 85B, p. 263). From this we might reasonably presume that even before being fully awake in devachan, one can become aware of the higher thoughts and feelings of those left behind. No devachanee can descend into our plane; it is awake in devachan. K.H. says: "*They* [the dead] *can be visited in Spirit*, their Spirit cannot descend and reach us. They attract, they cannot be attracted" (ML, letter 18, p. 63). H.P.B. tells us: "The only possible means of communicating with Devachanees is during sleep by a dream or vision. . . . No Devachanee can descend into our plane; it is for us—or rather our *inner Self*—to ascend to his" (CW 10:262).

Recently a gentleman in New York reported an experience that was likely a vision of someone in devachan. His dear friend, Ros, had been dead for over a year when she suddenly appeared to him looking radiantly happy. He was seated in front of a computer and was most certainly not thinking of her, yet her image appeared to him. He was nearly certain that it was Ros and not his imagination, so he wrote to her sister, Elaine, who lived in the U.K. The two sisters had been exceedingly close, so he thought Elaine would want to know about the experience. As soon as she received the letter, Elaine contacted him to say that the letter came at "such an important time." She had been feeling so down about her sister and the letter cheered her up "no end." She told the man that Ros had always said she would let her know if she was all right after she died, but that "she would not have come to me that way because it would have frightened me, so she went to you." Elaine went on to say that Ros loved her home and had just renovated it before becoming terminally ill so she did not have a chance to enjoy it. Therefore, Elaine had been unable to sell the house. For over a year it stood exactly as it was when vacated by Ros. "Now," said Elaine, "I can sell the house." This report seems to be an instance where one in devachan, radiantly happy, could attract a living person because she wanted her sister to know she was all right.

As K.H. reported, there are exceptions to every rule, and one of these exceptions is suicide. Theoretically each of us has a purpose to fulfill during our lifetime. We come into this world to work out some of the karma of our past, and in so doing, develop inner strength by overcoming the challenges we meet. That purpose has been called "dharma." As the prophet wrote in Ecclesiastes, "There is a time to die." That time is when we complete our dharma, or at least as much of it as possible in this life. A fair number of those who have had a near-death experience report that they returned not because they wanted to return but because they knew they still had important work to do. They had not fulfilled their dharma.

Should we commit suicide before our dharma has been fulfilled, we kill only the physical body. K.H. says that suicides are "not dead" because they have only killed what he calls their "physical triad." We remain trapped in our personality, the *me*, and are unable to go on to our reward in devachan until such time as we would have died by natural causes. Moreover, those who commit suicide for emotional reasons have not solved their problems. They awaken in an even more intensely emotional state because to some extent, when alive, our bodies tend to buffer our emotions. Now free of the body, the emotions are felt in all their intensity. One who commits suicide because of intransigent physical pain would still remain earth-bound until the time they would have died naturally, but in all likelihood they would not suffer the intense emotional distress that would be experienced by the one who committed suicide for an emotional reason such as the loss of a lover.

Another exception to the rule is what K.H. calls "the *immediate* reincarnation of children and congenital idiots." He regards them as "failures of nature," and says we cannot

> call them the *identical* ex-personalities; *though the whole of the same life-principle and identically the same* MANAS (fifth principle) *re-enters a new body* and may be truly called a 'reincarnation of the *personality*.' . . . All we can say of the reincarnated 'failures' is, that they are the reincarnated *Manas*, the fifth principle of Mr. Smith or Miss Grey, but certainly not that these are the reincarnations of Mr. S. and Miss G. (ML, letter 93B, p. 328)

So it is with all of us. The personality of Ed, Mary, Jack, or Jane does not reincarnate. What the inner self (the higher mind, or buddhi-manas) has been able to absorb and the lessons learned through incarnation will not be lost. Those lessons will be ingrained in our character throughout future incarnations. A simple example may help us to see how this may be true. Let us assume that as we are about to leave a theater we notice a woman who is walking away without her purse. Instantly, we call out, "Miss! You forgot your purse." We don't let the woman go and then steal the purse. The fact that stealing is against the law is not the reason we don't steal. It would be against our nature to steal. The lesson we learned in a previous incarnation is now part of our character. Obviously, some have not learned that lesson.

In some cases transgender people may also fall into the category of immediate reincarnations. In one case, a transgender person in New Jersey was asked when he first thought of himself as a woman. Surprisingly, he said it was in the first grade. The boys had to change into shorts for their gym class, and when he got to the door of the boys' room he said to himself, "I can't go in there. I'm a woman." Is it possible that the little boy had been a woman but for some fluke of nature, and karma had reincarnated her in a male body? Homosexuality may not fit into this category at all. In such cases the causes may be nature, nurture, or both. At present we don't have enough information to determine why some people are either born homosexual or become homosexual later in life.

Although our life between incarnations in devachan is certainly not the nineteenth-century idea of a heaven filled with golden streets and angels playing harps, it is a blissful time for all but that relatively small group of people who have been intensely selfish and evil all their lives. Those who throughout life have knowingly harmed, tortured, and murdered others with no regard for anyone but themselves enter into a state of psychological suffering known as "*avitchi.*" It is not the hell of medieval Christianity, but it is the karma reaped by depraved souls who have not an ounce of good to their merit.

In considering these theories about life after death, and whether or not we can communicate with the dead, it is important to remember that when writing letters, K.H. is not acting as an adept, but as a man who can make mistakes. He even points out that sometimes he may confuse terms, especially those made up by Sinnett, and that a comma or a missing adjective might entirely change his meaning. In view of this, it is important that we keep an open mind and not take intransigent positions based on what was written more than a century ago. When each of us dies, the experience will almost certainly be different than we supposed.

Just as there are many theories about what happens to us after death, so there are many theories about reward or punishment for our actions here on earth. In Section 9 of *The Key to Theosophy* (p. 161), Blavatsky tells us that "Karmic punishment reaches the Ego only in its next incarnation. After death it receives only the reward for the unmerited sufferings endured during its past incarnation." If what the Masters say about karma and after-death states is true, then it stands to reason that the results of former physical action appear in the next life on the physical plane. Likewise, emotional and mental action would have a karmic effect there. Since after death only the most spiritual aspirations and thoughts of the personality can be absorbed by the inner self, then the karma created while we are identified with and acting from the lower nature could not affect us in our inner, spiritual nature.

Therefore, the karmic "seeds" created by our actions in life are said to "hang in the atmosphere," awaiting the reincarnating ego to which they gravitate, and attach to the new personality on rebirth. In one sense we *are* our past karma. When K.H. resumed his correspondence after returning from his "retreat," he wrote, "Your *Karma* is your *only* personality to be when you step beyond" (ML, letter 47, p. 131). Furthermore, K.H. once said that the body of an adept is his conscious creation, whereas the body of the ordinary person is his unconscious creation. This implies that our bodies and no doubt our personalities are the results of personal karma. The adept, having neutralized personal karma, is able to "create" his own body, free from karmic seeds.

In reliving our life as we die, we get some sense of its purpose. Perhaps that is why the dying person often smiles at the moment of death. Finally, we understand the why of our life. The final review and summation of our life comes automatically and it largely determines the circumstances of our next birth. The Master assures us that there is no need to fear what thoughts might come to us at the moment of death:

> Such thoughts are *involuntary* and we have no more control over them than we would over the eye's retina to prevent it perceiving that colour which affects it most. At the last moment, the whole life is reflected in our memory and emerges from all the forgotten nooks and corners picture after picture, one event after the other. The dying brain dislodges memory with a strong supreme impulse, and memory restores faithfully every impression entrusted to it during the period of the brain's activity. That impression and thought which was the strongest naturally becomes the most vivid and survives so to say all the rest which now vanish and disappear for ever, to reappear but in Devachan. K.H. adds that the past is "casting its reflection upon the Veil of the Future." (ML, letter 93B, p. 326)

To get some sense of the process of reincarnation, we might consider the fact that the five-year-old child we all once were is dead forevermore. It will never reincarnate. Yet, the experience of that child has been "absorbed" by our consciousness. There is a continuity of consciousness, but not of the personality that our consciousness has informed.

Chapter 8

SCIENCE

Through most of the nineteenth century, scientists were confident that nearly all of the mysteries of the universe had been solved. They thought there were just a few things to tidy up. A chairman of the physics department at Harvard actually discouraged students from further research because he believed there was little of importance that they could discover. The French chemist Marcellin Berthelot wrote that the world of his day was now "without mystery," and the scientist Albert A. Michelson believed that any possibility of new scientific discoveries was "exceedingly remote." All had been solved. Scientists were convinced that everything in existence consisted of hard billiard-ball-like atoms that could not be split. Yet, in defiance of the science of her day, Madame Blavatsky maintained that the atom was not the hard, indivisible ball that the science of her times still claimed. She wrote that "the atom is divisible, and must consist of particles, or of *sub*-atoms." She then applies the same argument to the sub-atoms, and so on. She concludes: "But infinite divisibility of atoms resolves matter into simple centers of force, i.e., precludes the possibility of conceiving matter as an *objective* substance" (SD 1:519).

It was not until the late 1890s, and J. J. Thomson's work on cathode rays, which confirmed the existence of the electron, that it was realized by scientists that the atom is indeed divisible. Then, following experiments done at Cambridge in 1911, Lord Rutherford's so-called planetary atom won out over its rivals. This model proposed a number of outer electrons circulating around a central nucleus. Later, the nucleus itself was found to be made up of positive protons and neutral neutrons. Later again, it was found that protons and neutrons themselves possessed structure, the proton having two "up" quarks and a "down" quark, while the neutron has one "up" and two "down."

In addition to insisting that the atom was divisible, H.P.B. made some other startling predictions about the future of science. Among them is the statement from the *Secret Doctrine* that:

one by one facts and processes in Nature's workshops are permitted to find their way into the exact Sciences, while mysterious help is given to rare individuals in unravelling its arcana. It is at the close of great Cycles . . . that such events generally take place. We are at the very close of the cycle of 5,000 years of the present Aryan Kaliyuga; and between this time and 1897 there will be a large rent made in the Veil of Nature, and materialistic science will receive a deathblow. (SD 1:612)

On December 28, 1895, the first blow to materialistic science was delivered by Wilhelm Conrad Roentgen, who accidentally discovered X rays. One of his first X-ray photographs was of the bones in his wife's hand. The rays had penetrated an opaque object, passing through the hand as easily as sunlight passes through a window. A year later, Henri Becquerel discovered radioactivity, a radiation that can be deflected by a magnetic field. To cap off these remarkable discoveries, while following up on the work of Sir William Crookes on cathode rays, J. J. Thomson discovered the electron. The atom did consist of particles, as H.P.B. had said. Nineteenth-century science had been dealt a mortal blow, but it would take longer for it to evolve, and even now the philosophical implications of those discoveries have eluded both the public and most scientists.

Although the adepts disagreed with much of nineteenth-century science, they said "science is our best ally" (ML, letter 65, p. 168). K.H. wrote a letter summarizing the views of his superior, the Maha Chohan:

The doctrine we promulgate being the only true one must, supported by such evidence as we are preparing to give, become ultimately triumphant as every other truth. Yet it is absolutely necessary to inculcate it gradually, enforcing its theories, unimpeachable facts for those who know, with direct inferences deduced from and corroborated by the evidence furnished by modern exact science. (LMW1:2)

The Masters knew that matter was not composed of hard, billiard-ball–like atoms as physicists of the nineteenth century believed it to be. They hoped that future discoveries would lead to replacing such materialistic theories by revealing what Blavatsky called "the illusive nature of matter and the infinite divisibility of the atom" (SD 1:520). Since the higher classes of educated people trusted science, modern science was and still is the Masters' best ally.

Blavatsky was convinced that twentieth-century science would corroborate much of what was written in *The Secret Doctrine*. Amazingly, physics in part did just that. The materialistic theory about matter was challenged by Einstein, who theorized that matter is those regions of space in which the field (a nonmaterial reality) has become intense. He asserted that there is no room in the new physics for both matter and the field, because the field is the only reality.

The adepts accept nothing without first verifying it for themselves. Even if one of their Brotherhood should present new evidence for a theory, the others must verify it before accepting the evidence as valid. They say their science is "preeminently the science of effects by their causes and of causes by their effects" (ML, letter 88, p. 269). When it comes to physical science, the Masters admit that Western science is ahead of them, but claim they are ahead of the West in spiritual science. K.H. wrote: "You may be, and most assuredly are our superiors in every branch of physical knowledge; in spiritual sciences we were, are and always will be your—MASTERS" (ML, letter 11, p. 34). The term *spiritual sciences* may jar upon Western ears, but K.H. assures Sinnett that "occult science has its own methods of research as fixed and arbitrary as the methods of its antithesis physical science are in their way. If the latter has its dicta so also has the former" (ML, letter 2, p. 6).

The Secret Doctrine, Blavatsky's major work, treats both cosmogenesis (the origin of the universe) and anthropogenesis (the origin of the human species). Although H.P.B. is the principal author of that work, K.H. and Morya dictated part of it and gave their approval for most of the rest of it. About one fourth of *The Secret Doctrine* is dedicated to science. Perhaps it is that fact that has led some prominent scientists to join the Theosophical Society, or at least to read and admire portions if not the whole of *The Secret Doctrine*.

A niece of Einstein's reported that he kept a copy of *The Secret Doctrine* on his desk; and in an article entitled, "I Visit Professor Einstein," Jack Brown reports the same. Sir William Crookes, who discovered radiant matter, was a member of the Society. K.H. wrote of him, saying, "Crookes—has he not brought science within our hail in his 'radiant matter' discovery? What but occult research was it that *led* him first to that" (ML, letter 48, p. 134). Thomas Edison was also a member of the Society, and today there are members who are scientists and members who have an intense interest in science. The Society has no dogmas and it does not regard *The Secret Doctrine* as infallible holy writ, but it does encourage members and the public to consider the ideas presented in Theosophical literature.

Sylvia Cranston, the author of *H.P.B.: The Extraordinary Life and Influence of Helena Blavatsky*, reports that when nineteenth-century anthropologists were claiming that humanity on our planet was only several hundred thousand years old, H.P.B. claimed it was millions of years old. Today anthropologists agree that humanity is far older than they first thought. In addition to teaching that the nature of matter is not what it seems to be, Blavatsky taught that space is not empty. In fact, she said, there is no vacuity anywhere. Moreover, the atom has been discovered to be divisible, and scientists now claim that space is filled with virtual particles.

In another example of prescience, the Master K.H. told Sinnett: "Science will *hear* sounds from certain planets before she *sees* them. This is a *prophecy*" (ML, letter 93B, p. 325). We now have radio astronomy, and although we cannot hear planets with the naked ear, we can hear them if infrared and other waves are converted so as to be heard through a loudspeaker. We may note that K.H. may have meant stars when he said planets, but in any case, we can hear both with the proper instruments.

Some scientists have speculated that there might be other solar systems in the universe, whereas the Masters have declared it to be a fact. K.H. wrote: "If our greatest adepts and Bodhisattvas have never penetrated themselves beyond our solar system . . . they still know of the existence of other such solar systems, with as mathematical a certainty as any western astronomer knows of the existence of invisible stars which he can never approach or explore" (ML, letter 90, p. 280).

Commenting further, K.H. wrote:

> No planets but one have hitherto been discovered outside of the solar system, with all their photometers, while we know with the sole help of our spiritual *naked* eye a number of them; every *completely matured* Sun-star having, like in our own system, several companion planets in fact. (ML, letter 93B, p. 322)

These statements by K.H. were a prediction of what we call "exoplanets," and we now know there are more than a thousand of them.

The doctrine of ultimate unity and the doctrine of karma both suggest that everything is interconnected. Certainly the Masters taught that, and although we cannot say that either ultimate unity or karma has been proven scientifically, we can offer one piece of evidence that everything is interconnected, and not just by physical means.

The first hint that things are interconnected came with Heisenberg's Uncertainty Principle in 1927. On the quantum level, it was found to be impossible to measure a particle's property without changing the very thing you wanted to measure—the observer was part of the system observed. But interconnectedness goes even further. The quantum phenomenon of entanglement or nonlocality was something that Einstein could never accept, and some scientists still do not accept it. Einstein called it "spooky action at a distance." For entangled quantum particles, no matter how far apart they are, a change in the properties of one immediately and instantaneously brings about the same change in the other, something that seemed to challenge relativity.

The reality of this interconnectedness was finally demonstrated in 1981 by Alain Aspect and his colleagues working in Paris, by applying a theorem published in 1964 by Irish physicist John Bell. Quantum mechanics was proved valid—"spooky action at a distance" really does happen. The poet Francis Thompson (1859–1907) seems to have intuitively realized that when, in his poem "The Mistress of Vision," lines 33–34, he wrote that we cannot "stir a flower / Without troubling of a star."

From 1895 until 1933, Annie Besant and Charles W. Leadbeater claimed to have carried out clairvoyant investigations into the structure of atoms and subatomic particles. In 1995, the physicist Stephen M. Phillips published a book entitled *Extra-Sensory Perception of Quarks*, in which he theorized that the investigations of Besant and Leadbeater, published in their book *Occult Chemistry*, seemed to show that they had discovered quarks. In a second book, *The ESP of Quarks and Superstrings* (1999), Phillips suggested that the two clairvoyant investigators had also discovered the superstrings of modern string theory. So far as we know, the Masters never commented on the Besant–Leadbeater investigations. Clairvoyant investigation, however, is undoubtedly one of the tools used by the Masters in what they call "occult science."

Nineteenth-century scientists theorized that the universe

came into being by what H.P.B. called "a fortuitous concurrence of atoms" (SD 1:viii), and that at the core of every atom there was a hard, indivisible nucleus. It is a theory that was mocked in a joke about a scientist who had an exquisite model of the solar system. One of his scientific colleagues saw it one day and remarked on its beauty and accuracy. He then asked, "Who made it?" And his friend responded, "Oh, nobody. It just happened."

Christian clergy claim that God created the universe. Although today mainstream Christianity takes a less literal view of the creation story and of scripture in general, the literal view was common among both clergy and people in the nineteenth century. One of the problems with the literal theory is that chapters 1 and 2 of the book of Genesis have different versions of the creation. In the first chapter, God creates human beings first, both male and female, and without taking a rib from Adam. In the second chapter, God seems to create along lines similar to the theory of evolution by starting with the earth and working up to human beings.

Rejecting creation theories, the adepts say that order is embedded in the very nature of the universe. It is not an order imposed upon it by an extra-cosmic God. In *The Secret Doctrine*, H.P.B. claims that "everything in the universe, as well as the universe itself, is formed . . . by accelerated MOTION set into activity by . . . the ever-to-be-unknown power" (SD 2:551–552).

According to esoteric philosophy, motion is not meaningless. It displays order and purpose in whatever state it is found. The second fundamental proposition of *The Secret Doctrine* asserts the absolute universality of that law of periodicity, of flux and reflux, ebb and flow, which physical science has observed and recorded in all departments of nature. An alternation such as that of Day and Night, Life and Death, Sleeping and Waking, is a fact so common, so perfectly universal and without exception, that it is easy to comprehend that in it we see one of the absolutely fundamental laws of the universe. (SD 1:17)

Such cycles are evident everywhere in the objective world and even in subjective states. Our emotions and our mind are never still. They switch between active and passive over and over again. Cycles, at least in the physical world, are ordered motion.

According to *The Secret Doctrine*, motion is creative. Perhaps no better example of the creative power of motion can be found than in the example of H_2O, of which steam, water, and ice are all different states. Yet these three states of the same substance are radically different in appearance. If we asked a friend for H_2O in the summer, we would probably mean a glass of cold water. If our friend gave us a blast of steam instead, he would no longer be our friend. Our friend, however, would have done as we asked, given us H_2O, but not in the state we wanted it to be. What is the essential difference among steam, water, and ice? The answer to that question is simply their rate of motion. Exceedingly rapid motion of H_2O produces steam, less rapid motion produces water, and a still slower rate of motion produces ice. These three are one, but each is in a different state of that one substance.

Analogously, the universe is thought to be substantially the same. All creatures and things are different states of the ONE. K.H. wrote: "Every grain of sand, every boulder or crag of granite is that spirit crystallized or petrified" (ML, letter 67, p. 183). Einstein postulated a theory that seems close to what K.H. said about matter being crystallized spirit. He said that matter is "constituted by the regions of space in which the field is extremely intense." He went on to say, "There is no place in this new physics for both the field and matter, for the field is the only reality" (cited in Nicholson, *Ancient Wisdom: Modern Insight*, p. 45). In other words, the material world is but a state of the nonmaterial reality.

The third fundamental proposition of *The Secret Doctrine* can be summarized in one word: *evolution*. The Theosophical theory of evolution, however, is not the now somewhat out-of-date Darwinian theory. From a Theosophical perspective, we might think of ultimate reality as a universal, dynamic force field. That field "molds" matter in a way similar to the way in which the field of a bar magnet "molds" iron filings on a paper. The filings reveal the lines of force from the field. Yet the field itself is nonmaterial. No one has ever seen a field or ever will. We know that fields exist only from the way that matter behaves in their presence. The ultimate unified field might be consciousness itself, ever changing, living, and molding matter to reveal its nature.

Master Morya tried to explain something of his theory of the emergence of the universe to Sinnett. He explained that the adepts did not accept the idea of a creator God. Rather, he wrote:

Go on saying: "Our planet and man were created"—and you will be fighting against *hard facts* for ever, analyzing and losing time over trifling details—unable to ever grasp the whole. But once admit that our planet and ourselves are no more *creations* than the iceberg now before me (in our K.H.'s home) but that both planet and man are—*states* for a given time; that their present appearance—geological and anthropological—is transitory and but a condition concomitant of that stage of evolution at which they have arrived in the descending cycle—and all will become plain. (ML, letter 44, pp. 119–120)

Chapter 9

WORKING TO
MOLD THE FUTURE

Some have said that one of the last mysteries to be solved is that of time. Physicists theorize that there was no chronological time before the big bang. Chronological time is dependent on motion. If our earth was not moving around the sun, we would not have the time segments we call "years."

St. Augustine was intrigued by the mystery of time. He mused that he could not measure the future because it was not yet, and he could not measure the past because it was no longer. Then he realized that he could not measure the present because no sooner had he measured it than it was in the past. The conclusion was that one cannot measure time.

The Masters say that there is only an eternal now. But that "now" is beyond what we call time. The word K.H. uses for it is *duration*. In her *Secret Doctrine* (1:27), H.P.B. quoted the second verse of the Stanzas of Dzyan: "Time was not, for it lay asleep in the infinite bosom of duration." Almost certainly she was describing a state before the big bang.

Writing in English, K.H. became frustrated with the usual words describing time. He wrote:

> I feel even irritated at having to use these three clumsy words—past, present and future! Miserable concepts of the objective phases of the Subjective Whole, they are about as ill adapted for the purpose as an axe for fine carving. (ML, letter 15, p. 46)

We human beings are so bound by the clock that we do not realize that while motion and cycles (ordered motion) are real, time is an illusion. Past, present, and future all exist now. The present is the result of what we call the past. The past exists only in our memory, and as psychologists well know, many of our psychological problems arise because we live in the memory of events. The future exists only as potential action. We can change the future by acting now.

Let us imagine that we are driving on a highway. We see that ahead of us there has been an accident and police have reduced the four-lane road to just one lane. We are traveling at sixty miles an hour when we see the block. At that moment, the future potential is to crash through the roadblock, no doubt causing severe damage or even death. We can change that future potential, however, by slowing down.

To a certain extent the Masters can predict future events by calculating the likely effects of current potential, and they have dedicated themselves to molding the future to help humanity avoid disastrous events that would occur unless people and nations changed their course. The Masters never force people to do anything, but they do try to inspire people to move in a right direction. Some of the greater adepts can see the future more easily than others. In a letter to Olcott, K.H. reports that to his superior, the Maha Chohan, "the future lies like an open page" (LMW1:41). Because of their deep concern for humanity as a whole, their influence extends not only to individuals, but also to nations.

In 1880, the Theosophical Society was undergoing one of the many crises it would endure throughout its existence, this time over the backlash from an article Olcott had written entitled "A Day with Madame Blavatsky." In the article, Olcott described some of the amazing phenomena produced by H.P.B. at Simla. Unfortunately, he mentioned the names of some prominent Englishmen who were present to witness it. The *Times of India* got hold of the article and published it, along with some damning commentary that caused great embarrassment to the Englishmen mentioned in the article. The whole thing boomeranged on H.P.B., and as might be expected of her, she became so frantic that she practically screamed for help from the Master K.H.

In the same year there was another, far greater and more important crisis that was coming to a head on the border of Tibet. K.H. wrote:

A crisis, in a certain sense, is upon us now, and must be met. I might say two crises—one, the Society's, the other for

Tibet. For, I may tell you in confidence, that Russia is gradually massing her forces for a future invasion of that country under the pretext of a Chinese war. If she does not succeed it will be due to us; and herein, at least we will deserve your gratitude. You see then, that we have weightier matters than small societies to think about; yet, the T.S. must not be neglected. (ML, letter 5, p. 15)

It is important to notice the phrase, "*If* she does not succeed." The Masters try to influence people, but they never block individuals from choosing how they will respond to that influence.

In another crisis in Egypt, K.H. reported that the physical presence of some adepts might be required to neutralize the problem. It is not clear what the crisis was, but K.H. described it this way:

Just now I am able to give you a bit of information, which bears upon the so often discussed question of our allowing phenomena. The Egyptian operations of your blessed countrymen [the English] involve such local consequences to the body of Occultists still remaining there and to what they are guarding, that two of our adepts are already there, having joined some Druze brethren, and three more on their way. . . . For such great emergency is our Force stored up, and hence— we dare not waste it on fashionable tamasha [entertainment]. (ML, letter 68, p. 203)

Although A. O. Hume had witnessed some remarkable phenomena, allegedly produced by the adepts, he accused them of failing to leave a mark on human history. Responding to the challenge, K.H. wrote:

> How do you know they [the adepts] have made no such mark? Are you acquainted with their efforts, successes, and failures? . . . What they have done they know; all those outside their circle could perceive was results, the causes of which were masked from view. . . . There never was a time within or before the so-called historical period when our predecessors were not moulding events and "making history," the facts of which were subsequently and invariably distorted by "historians" to suit contemporary prejudices. Are you quite sure that the visible heroic figures in the successive dramas were not often but their puppets?

And then reaffirming the position that the adepts are not omnipotent, K.H. adds, "We never pretended to be able to draw nations in the mass to this or that crisis in spite of the general drift of the world's cosmic relations" (ML, first letter of K.H. to A. O. Hume, pp. 473–474).

Chapter 10

FOUNDING OF THE THEOSOPHICAL SOCIETY

When Koot Hoomi and Morya decided to launch the experiment that became the Theosophical Society, they had little support from their fellow adepts. K.H. wrote: "my Brother and I are the only among the Brotherhood who have at heart the dissemination (to a certain limit) of our doctrines" (ML, letter 131, p. 435). He had earlier observed: "None of my Fellow Brothers with the exception of M. will help me in this work, not even our semi-European Greek Brother [the Master Hilarion]" (ML, letter 65, p. 169). Apparently, the other Masters were reluctant to approve the experiment because they doubted it would work. Nevertheless, despite their skepticism, the Brotherhood finally gave K.H. and Morya permission to begin the experiment, but some strict rules were imposed. Morya wrote: "It was stipulated, however, that the experiment should be made independently of our personal management;

that there should be no abnormal interference by ourselves" (ML, letter 45, p. 125).

Unfortunately, although the Society is dedicated to universal brotherhood, it has been plagued with internecine strife since its founding. As one T.S. member once put it: "No people. No problems." But there *are* people, and members of the Society are not exempt from human weakness. It is alleged that, during one of the difficult periods of the early T.S., a member asked one of the adepts why he did not intervene to solve the problems. The adept answered that by not intervening they could see who stood for principles and who for personalities. K.H. made the essential purpose of the Theosophical Society clear to Sinnett early on in their correspondence. He wrote: "The *Chiefs* want a 'Brotherhood of Humanity,' a real Universal Fraternity started; an institution which would make itself known throughout the world and arrest the attention of the highest minds" (ML, letter 12, p. 39).

In the 1880s, the idea of a universal brotherhood of humanity was not popular, and neither Sinnett nor Hume was fond of the idea. No matter what K.H. said about universal brotherhood, Sinnett resisted the concept. He much preferred a school of occultism for the elite few. K.H. was aware of that and wrote to Sinnett that:

> you have ever discussed but to put down the idea of a universal Brotherhood, questioned its usefulness, and advised to remodel the T.S. on the principle of a college for the special study of occultism. This, my respected and esteemed friend and Brother—will never do! (ML, letter 2, p. 8)

Then explaining why he thought universal brotherhood so important he wrote: "The term 'Universal Brotherhood' is no idle phrase. Humanity in the mass has a paramount claim upon us. . . . It is the only secure foundation for universal morality. If it be a dream, it is at least a noble one for mankind: and it is the aspiration of the *true adept*" (ML, letter 5, p. 20). Koot Hoomi further told Sinnett:

> The truths and mysteries of occultism constitute, indeed, a body of the highest spiritual importance, at once profound and practical for the world at large. Yet, it is not as a mere addition to the tangled mass of theory or speculation in the world of science that they are being given to you, but for their practical bearing on the interests of mankind . . . *constructive* of new institutions of a genuine, practical Brotherhood of Humanity where all will become co-workers of nature, will work for the good of mankind. (ML, letter 12, pp. 38–39)

The Masters wanted the Theosophical Society and its members to "popularize" Theosophy for the benefit of humanity, not for the benefit of a few elite. In an abridged version of the view of the Maha Chohan, K.H.'s superior, the adept wrote:

> For our doctrines to practically react on the so-called moral code, or the ideas of truthfulness, purity, self-denial, charity, etc., we have to preach and popularise a knowledge of theosophy. It is not the individual and determined purpose of attaining oneself Nirvana (the culmination of all knowledge

and absolute wisdom) which is, after all only an exalted and glorious *selfishness*, but the self-sacrificing pursuit of the best means to lead on the right path our neighbour, to cause as many of our fellow-creatures as we possibly can to benefit by it, which constitutes the true theosophist. . . . To achieve the proposed object, a greater, wiser, and especially a more benevolent intermingling of the high and the low, of the alpha and the omega of society, was determined upon. The white race must be the first to stretch out the hand of fellowship to the dark nations, to call the poor despised "nigger" brother. This prospect may not smile to all. He is no Theosophist who objects to this principle. (LMW1:3–4)

As mentioned previously, from almost the day it was founded, the Theosophical Society was plagued with internecine strife. The first major conflict was when W. Q. Judge fell out with H. S. Olcott and Annie Besant. As is almost always the case in disputes, there are two sides to the story, and perhaps a third which is the truth. Whatever the truth might be, Judge told Annie Besant that if she went to Adyar, Olcott would poison her. Olcott mentions the warning in his *Old Diary Leaves* (4:525). He wrote:

And to think that while writing . . . to Mrs. Besant that I might try to poison her, he [Judge] had the audacity to say in his official report to our Convention of 1892. . . . The American Section therefore offers to you the reiterated assurances of its loyalty and its determination to cooperate with you and every other member of every Section in carrying forward the work of the Society until we shall have passed away, and others arisen to take our places in the forward movement.

In 1895, Judge ended the controversy by declaring the American Section independent and withdrawing it from the parent body. In 1896, just one year after his secession, Judge died. He was succeeded in his organization by Katherine Tingley, a woman whom he had met in New York in 1894 and who had become a Theosophist almost immediately after meeting Judge. Tingley named the breakaway society in America "The Universal Brotherhood and Theosophical Society." Since then, several other Theosophical groups have been formed. Human nature being what it is, when two or more people come together there are sure to be at least three strongly held and divergent opinions. Even before these splits, K.H. and Morya almost despaired of the Theosophical Society, saying that perhaps their fellow adepts were right when they expressed strong doubts that the experiment of teaching Westerners something of their philosophy would succeed.

In an effort to salvage the heart of the Theosophical Society, Blavatsky wanted to create a separate section of the Society known as the Esoteric Section. She hoped that would gather together some *true* Theosophists through whom the Society might still fulfill its purpose. When Olcott learned of this new section, he strenuously objected to it. He believed so strongly in the idea of universal brotherhood and equality that he thought establishing a separate "elite" section of the Theosophical Society would violate those principles. To put it mildly, Olcott was angry with H.P.B. and he intended to have it out with her. At the time, H.P.B. was in Europe, and while Olcott was on a ship to London to meet with her, a letter from K.H. was precipitated to him in his cabin. (Those who claim that all of the precipitated letters were fraudulently produced by H.P.B. will be hard pressed to explain how she managed that from Europe.)

In his letter, K.H. wrote:

But your revolt, good friend, against her infallibility—as you once thought it—has gone too far and you have been unjust to her. . . . Just now, on deck, your thoughts about her were dark and sinful, and so I find the moment a fitting one to put you on your guard . . . we employ agents—the best available. Of these for the past thirty years the chief has been the personality known as H.P.B. to the world (but otherwise to us). Imperfect and very troublesome, no doubt, she proves to some, nevertheless, there is no likelihood of our finding a better one for years to come—and your theosophists should be made to understand it.

K.H. went on to contrast Olcott's role with Blavatsky's:

H.P.B. has next to no concern with administrative details, and should be kept clear of them, so far as her strong nature can be controlled. But this *you must tell to all:—With occult matters she has everything to do.* . . . She is *our direct agent.* I warn you against permitting your suspicions and resentment against "her many follies" to bias your intuitive loyalty to her. In the adjustment of this European business, you will have two things to consider—the external and administrative, and the internal and psychical. Keep the former under your control and that of your most prudent associates, jointly: *leave the latter to her.* You are left to devise the practical details with your usual ingenuity. Only be careful, I say, to discriminate . . . between that which is merely exoteric in origin and effects, and that which beginning on the practical tends to beget consequences on the spiritual plane. As to the former you are the best judge, as to the latter, she. (LMW1:44–46)

As a result of the letter, Olcott changed his mind about the formation of the Esoteric Section. He persuaded H.P.B. to create the Esoteric Section as an independent organization, however, rather than as an integral part of the Theosophical Society. Today it is known as the Esoteric School of Theosophy. While remaining independent, however, the ES draws its members exclusively from the Theosophical Society. To apply for membership in the ES, one must have been a member of the Theosophical Society in good standing for at least two years. Members of the ES must also be vegetarians, nonsmokers, and nondrinkers, and they must abstain from drugs other than those prescribed by a doctor.

Chapter 11

ALLEGED ENCOUNTERS
WITH MASTERS

In the late 1800s, no fewer than twenty-five to thirty-five people claimed to have met a Master, in either the physical or the astral body. Some of these claims seem so fantastic that one might judge them false. Others have the ring of truth to them. One case in particular is that of Colonel Olcott, who reports that the Master Morya appeared to him in New York at the apartment he shared with H.P.B. on West Forty-seventh Street and Eighth Avenue. The press had dubbed their apartment the "Lamasary." Olcott reports that he saw Morya in his astral body when it materialized before his very eyes. Morya's real body remained in Tibet, but he "projected" a duplicate of himself to the Lamasary in order to converse directly with Olcott. The apparition was so amazing that Olcott's account of it is worth reading almost in its entirety.

I was quietly reading, with all my attention centered on my book. Nothing in the evening's incidents had prepared me for seeing an adept in his astral body; I had not wished for it, tried to conjure it up in my fancy, nor in the least expected it. All at once, as I read with my shoulder a little turned from the door, there came a gleam of something white in the right-hand corner of my right eye; I turned my head, dropped my book in astonishment, and saw towering above me in his great stature an Oriental clad in white garments, and wearing a head-cloth or turban of amber-striped fabric, hand-embroidered in yellow floss-silk. Long raven hair hung from under his turban to the shoulders; his black beard, parted vertically on the chin in the Rajput fashion, was twisted up at the ends and carried over the ears; his eyes were alive with soul-fire; eyes which were at once benignant and piercing in glance; the eyes of a mentor and a judge, but softened by the love of a father who gazes on a son needing counsel and guidance. He was so grand a man, so imbued with the majesty of moral strength, so luminously spiritual, so evidently above average humanity, that I felt abashed in his presence, and bowed my head and bent my knee as one does before a god or a god-like personage. A hand was lightly laid on my head, a sweet though strong voice bade me be seated, and when I raised my eyes, the Presence was seated in the other chair beyond the table. He told me he had come at the crisis when I needed him; that my actions had brought me to this point; that it lay with me alone whether he and I should meet often in this life as co-workers for the good of mankind; that a great work was to be done for humanity, and I had the right to share in it if I wished; that a mysterious tie, not now to be explained to me, had drawn my colleague and myself together; a tie which could not be broken, however strained it might be at times. He told me things about H.P.B. that I may not repeat, as well as things about myself, that do not concern third parties. How long he was there I cannot tell: it might have been a half-hour or an hour; it seemed but a minute, so little did I take note of the flight of time. At last he rose, I wondering at his great height and observing the sort of splendour in his countenance—not an external shining, but the soft gleam, as it were, of an inner light—that of the spirit. Suddenly the thought came into my mind: "What if this be but hallucination; what if H.P.B. has cast a hypnotic glamour over me? I wish I had some tangible object to prove to me that he has really been here; something that I might handle after he is gone!" The Master smiled kindly as if reading my thought, untwisted the *fehtá* from his head, benignantly saluted me in farewell and—was gone: his chair was empty; I was alone with my emotions! Not quite alone, though, for on the table lay the embroidered head-cloth; a tangible and enduring proof that I had not been "overlooked," or psychically befooled, but had been face to face with one of the Elder Brothers of Humanity, one of the Masters of our dull pupil-race / . . . I have been blessed with meetings with this Master and others since then, but little profit is to be reaped in repeating tales of experiences of which the foregoing is a sufficient example. However others less fortunate may doubt, I KNOW. (Olcott, *Old Diary Leaves* 1:379–381)

The turban that Morya left is now at the Theosophical Society headquarters in Adyar.

Olcott claims to have had several other encounters with the Masters, but he is by no means alone in such claims. Daniel H. Caldwell reports that no less than twenty-five people during H.P.B.'s lifetime testified to seeing one or more of the Mahatmas. Among his reports are the following:

On July 13, 1881, Bhavani Shankar claims that he, Madame Blavatsky, Monsieur Coulomb, Madame Coulomb, and a few others saw K.H. for a few minutes at some distance in his "*mayavi rupa,*" or double. Shankar said the Master was dressed in a Punjabee outfit and that he wore a white turban. K.H. then appeared to them again, but at a distance of only a yard or two. Shankar said that K.H. then went to Blavatsky's room and all heard him conversing with her. Everyone present saw the Master, and all agreed to draft and sign a letter to the *London Spiritualist* about the experience. Shankar adds, "Since Madame Coulomb now says that the Mahatmas are but 'crafty arrangements of muslin and bladders' and her husband represented the Mahatmas, how are we to reconcile this statement with the fact that in the *London Spiritualist* of the 19th August 1881, appeared a letter signed by five witnesses, including myself, testifying to the fact of their having seen a Mahatma, while they were writing that letter; and that this document is signed by both the Coulombs? There is, therefore, no doubt that they were with the company who signed the paper. Who was it then that appeared on that occasion as a Mahatma? Surely neither Monsieur and Madame Coulomb with their 'muslin and bladders' nor Madame B.'s servant who was also present, but the 'double' of a person living on the other side of the Himalayas." (Theosophical Society, *Report of the Result of an Investigation into the Charges against Madame Blavatsky Brought by the Missionaries of the Scottish Free Church of Madras, and Examined by a Committee Appointed for That Purpose by the General Council of the Theosophical Society* [Madras, India: Theosophical Society, 1885], 75–80)

In August 1881, Damodar K. Mavalankar gave the following testimony:

I have at least seen about half a dozen [Brothers] on various occasions, in broad daylight, in open places, and have talked to them, not only when Madame Blavatsky was in Bombay but even when she was far away and I here. I have also seen them . . . when I was travelling. I was taken to the residences of some of them and once when Colonel Olcott and Madame Blavatsky were with me. Further than that I cannot say, and shall not give any more information either about them or the places they reside in, for I am under a solemn obligation of secrecy and the subject is too sacred for me to be trifled with. I may, however, mention that I know "Koot Hoomi Lal Singh" personally and have seen and conversed with him when Madame Blavatsky was here as also when she was far away. . . . We Hindus who know the "Brothers" think it equally absurd and ridiculous to insinuate that either Madame Blavatsky is a lunatic or an impostor, or that persons like Mr. Sinnett could have ever become her dupes. Neither is she a medium, nor are the "Brothers" "disembodied Spirits." (Caldwell, *Casebook of Encounters*, Case 1, p. 16)

Another report of an encounter with a Master comes from Mirza Moorad Alee Beg, recorded in Bombay in August 1881.

Having just read in the London *Spiritualist* a review of Mr. Sinnett's book, "The Occult World," I find in it more than a doubt expressed as to the reality of the "Brothers," that body of mystics to which the personage known as "Koot Hoomi Lal Singh" belongs. . . . As some persons may express the same doubts, and also some, while admitting their genuine character, may attribute them to agency other than that to which Madame Blavatsky refers them (the so-called "Brothers," &c.), I hereby declare that not only have I within the last few days seen one of the persons so designated at the Headquarters of the Society at Bombay, but that I have very good reasons (which I cannot go into more fully now) to know that the said persons are not "spirits" but real human beings exercising powers out of the ordinary. Both before and after my connection with the Theosophical Society I have known and conversed with them personally and witnessed the most wonderful results (which would ordinarily be described as miraculous), but I must emphasise my declaration that I do not regard them as supernatural and am altogether materialistic (or rather naturalistic) in my conceptions of the agency producing them. Further I testify that I have the strongest conviction, based on reasons which, though authoritative, are purely natural and physical, that the said "Brothers" are a mysterious fraternity, the ordinary location of which is the regions north of the Himalayas. ("*The Occult World* and *The Spiritualist*," *Theosophist* 2 [August 1881]:230)

In 1883, William T. Brown claimed he met K.H. in the daylight when it would have been much more difficult for anyone to fool him by masquerading as a Master in "crafty arrangements of muslin and bladder." Brown reported, "On the afternoon of the 19th November, I saw the Master in broad daylight, and recognized him, and on the morning of the 20th he came to my tent, and said, 'Now you see me before you in the flesh; look and assure yourself that it is I,' and left a letter of instructions and silk handkerchief." Later in life it appears that Brown began to believe that instead of meeting with the Master he had been fooled as Madame Coulomb had charged. K.H. confirmed the visit, however, in a letter to Brown when he wrote:

If an Eastern, especially a Hindu, had even half a glimpse but once of what you had, he would have considered himself blessed the whole of his life. . . . You saw and recognized me twice at a distance, you knew it was I and no other; what more do you desire? (Brown, *Some Experiences in India* [London: London Lodge of the Theosophical Society, 1884])

In his book *The Masters and the Path* (pp. 8–9), C. W. Leadbeater describes his first encounter with one of the Masters. He writes:

> The door of the room was in full sight, and it certainly did not open; but quite suddenly, without any preparation, there was a man standing almost between me and Madame Blavatsky, within touch of both of us. It gave me a great start; and I jumped up in some confusion; Madame Blavatsky was much amused and said: "If you do not know enough not to be startled at such a trifle as that, you will not get far in this occult work."

In 1994, the State University of New York Press published a book by K. Paul Johnson entitled, *The Masters Revealed: Madame Blavatsky and the Myth of the Great White Lodge*. It is a scholarly book, and it is kind to Blavatsky. In his book, Johnson claims that Morya and Koot Hoomi, along with the other Masters mentioned by H.P.B., were basically fictionalized composites of historical men. Essentially, Johnson identifies the "Masters" as follows:

Serapis = Paolos Matamon
Tuitit Bey = Max Théon (L. M. Bimstein)
Hilarion = Ooton Liatto

Djual Khool = Dayal Singh
The Chohan = K.H. em Singh Bedi
Koot Hoomi = Thakar Singh
Morya = Ranbir Singh

Of particular interest are Koot Hoomi and Morya, the two adepts who allegedly wrote most of the letters to A. P. Sinnett and others. Ranbir Singh (allegedly Morya) was the Maharaja of Kashmir, and Thakar Singh (allegedly K.H.) was devoted to religious reform and the defense of Sikhism against the attacks from Christian missionaries. Johnson theorizes that Blavatsky may have taken the idea of secret masters from traditions with which she was familiar and then invented names for her "secret masters." Curiously, Johnson does not suggest that Thakar Singh, identified as K.H., wrote the letters to A. P. Sinnett and others. We might therefore reasonably ask, "Then who did write them?" According to handwriting experts from the British Museum and others in the twentieth century, whoever wrote them, it could not have been Blavatsky.

Letters from K.H. were still being received after the death of Thakar Singh, and at least one after the death of H.P.B., but since Johnson does not suggest that Singh wrote the letters, he does not address that issue. Moreover, he does not comment on a letter from K.H. concerning Blavatsky's visit with the Masters in Sikkim. K.H. wrote:

> I do not believe I was ever so profoundly touched by anything
> I witnessed in all my life, as I was with the poor old creature's

[Blavatsky's] ecstatic rapture, when meeting us recently both in our natural bodies, one—after three years, the other—nearly two years absence and separation in flesh. Even our phlegmatic M. was thrown off his balance by such an exhibition—of which he was chief hero. He had to use his *power*, and plunge her into a profound sleep, otherwise she would have burst some blood-vessel including kidneys, liver and her "interiors"—to use our friend Oxley's favourite expression—in her delirious attempts to flatten her nose against his riding mantle besmeared with the Sikkim mud! We both laughed; yet could we feel otherwise but touched? (ML, letter 92, p. 297)

To counteract the charges made that the Mahatmas were no more than what Madame Coulomb called "crafty arrangements of muslin and bladder," Mohini M. Chatterji, in February 1884, wrote:

Since an attempt is now being made by the opponents of the Theosophical Society to discredit the whole movement by circulating the report that the "Mahatmas," or Eastern Adepts, are but "crafty arrangements of muslin and bladders," I ask permission to say a word. I have sacrificed all my worldly prospects, as is well known in my native city of Calcutta, to devote myself to the propagation of the esoteric philosophy of my race, in connection with the Society so unjustly slandered. Needless to say I should not have taken this step, with many others of my countrymen, if the Theosophical Society were but a sham, and the Mahatmas vulgar "concoctions of muslin and bladders." To a Brahman, like myself, it is repugnant to speak of the sacredly confidential relationship existing between a spiritual teacher and his pupil yet duty compels me in this instance to say that I have personal and absolute knowledge of the existence of the Mahatma who has corresponded with Mr. Sinnett, and is known to the Western world as "Koot-Hoomi." I had knowledge of the Mahatma in question before I knew Mdme. Blavatsky, and I met him in person when he passed through the Madras Presidency to China last year. (Collated from "The Theosophical Mahatmas" by Mohini M. Chatterji, *The Pall Mall Gazette* [London], October 2, 1884, p. 2)

In the twentieth century and even today, some people claim to have contact with K.H., Morya, the Comte de Saint Germain, and other Masters. Although no one can prove the claims true or false, it is clear that the alleged encounters are often not at all like the Masters K.H. speaks of in the Mahatma Letters. Frequently the encounters seem to be with nonhuman spirits rather than with men of flesh and blood, as the adepts say they are. Also, even though the Masters strongly deny that they help people with their personal problems, many of the claims report that they do just that. In other cases, the adepts seem to have become nearly mystical Christians, contradicting K.H.'s claim that they are Buddhists in their philosophy if not in outward observance of Buddhist rites.

In 1919, Alice Bailey, a member of the Theosophical Society

and the Esoteric School, claimed she was contacted telepathically by the Master Djual Khool (D.K.), whom K.H. refers to in the Mahatma Letters as a high chela, not yet a Master at the time. For approximately the next thirty years, she wrote books of her own and also some she claimed D.K. dictated to her. Among the works she claimed D.K. dictated is a book entitled *The Reappearance of the Christ*, in which she makes Christ out to be a great adept or avatar. In contrast, K.H. taught that "the Christ of every preacher" is our sixth principle, buddhi, not an avatar or even a historical figure. As previously mentioned, K.H. also claimed that the Jesus of the Bible is a spiritual abstraction and not the real Jesus, who K.H. says is an adept. In *The Reappearance of the Christ*, Djual Khool seems to be more a mystical Christian than a Buddhist, and he clearly teaches a different doctrine than his Master, K.H. Obviously, one may choose to believe one or the other version of the Jesus/Christ story, or neither, but when the two teachings are contradictory, one cannot believe both.

In addition to the different teachings about the Christ, the Bailey books contain other material that is in direct contradiction to what the Mahatmas and Blavatsky have said. They also contain teachings that cannot be found in the primary literature. Bailey contradicts the Mahatma K.H. when she writes that initiates, and even Masters, fully participate in sexual relations in marriage. In her *Initiation, Human and Solar*, chapter 19, she says that many individuals have become initiates while participating in marital relations. She adds that often Masters marry and carry out all the duties of a husband or wife, but that their sexual relations are not driven by desire or passion. In direct contradiction to this idea, K.H. writes: "It is true that the married man cannot be an adept" (ML, letter 5, p. 19). The Masters do not think that all sexual relations are sinful or that we must be celibate to live a spiritual life. Rather, they know that sexual relations create personal ties, and personal ties create karma. They claim they have neutralized their own personal karma and they avoid creating any new karma that will bind them to others personally. Followers of Bailey claim that her material is a continuation of *The Secret Doctrine*. The many differences in the teachings and tone of *The Secret Doctrine* and the Bailey writings make that claim highly unlikely, especially as the two sometimes directly contradict each other.

Another alleged twentieth-century encounter with a Master is that of Guy Ballard, an American businessman who claimed he met the Comte de Saint Germain while hiking on Mount Shasta in California. As a result of the "revelations" he received from Saint Germain, he and his wife, Edna, founded the I AM movement, which was the first to call the adepts "Ascended Masters," and they were the first to put "El" in front of Morya's name and "Khan" after it. The group believes that the Ascended Masters are supernatural beings who have attained their status after many incarnations as human beings. Their pantheon includes Jesus, El Morya Khan, Maitreya, and about twenty others. Ballard has been reported to believe that in previous lives he had been George Washington, a well-known French musician, and an Egyptian priest. Ballard claimed to have received thousands of messages from Saint Germain, and those messages are the core of the group's study.

On August 7, 1958, Mark L. Prophet founded the Summit Lighthouse in Washington, D.C. The Summit Lighthouse publishes the teachings of the Church Universal and Triumphant, founded in 1975 by Elizabeth Clare Prophet, Mark's wife. The group claims to have received messages from many Masters who they believe have "ascended" out of humanity and become immortal. Based on a prediction that there would be nuclear war by the end of the decade, in 1989 the Church began to build fallout shelters at their location in Montana.

The descriptions of the Masters and their messages reported by these several groups have little or no connection with the Brothers of H. P. Blavatsky and others in the 1880s.

Chapter 12

FORGERY AND
PLAGIARISM

Despite strong evidence that Blavatsky did not forge the Mahatma Letters nor use trickery to manifest alleged adepts, many believed she was a fraud. One of the most upsetting charges of forgery and trickery came from Madame Coulomb.

In 1871, Blavatsky was on one of her periodic visits to the Middle East. She was in Cairo where she founded the Société Spirite, an organization she hoped would investigate and prove the reality of psychic phenomena. The Société lasted only two weeks and was dissolved by H.P.B. at its second meeting when a crowd discovered that a so-called medium was cheating. Miss Emma Cutting attended that second meeting and donated a small sum of money to Blavatsky's work. Madame Blavatsky soon left for Odessa, and Miss Cutting married Alexis Coulomb, a Frenchman whose family ran a hotel. In 1874, after the Coulombs attempted a fraudulent bankruptcy, they fled to

Calcutta, and from there to Ceylon (now Sri Lanka). Emma wrote to H.P.B. asking for a loan of two hundred rupees, but Blavatsky replied that all her funds were tied up in the work and she did not have the money to make a loan. To everyone's surprise, the Coulombs soon turned up at the Theosophical Society headquarters in Bombay "shoeless, penniless, and starving." In an act of kindness so typical of H.P.B., she invited the Coulombs to stay at the headquarters, where Emma would work as a housekeeper and Alexis as a handyman. In 1882, the Theosophical Society headquarters was moved to Adyar, Madras (now Chennai), and the Coulombs went, along with the others.

H.P.B. soon discovered that Emma Coulomb was slandering her behind her back, while flattering her to her face. After the discovery of Emma's plan to extort two thousand rupees from a wealthy Indian member, Emma vowed to do what harm she could to H.P.B. and to the Theosophical Society. She wasted no time in planning her revenge. She claimed that H.P.B. was the source of the Mahatma Letters and that K.H. and Morya were fictitious characters invented by Blavatsky. The alleged appearance of these Masters was created by masks and a "doll" head on a stick. In one case she said, "Madame's servant took the [doll], all wrapped up in a shawl, and with Mr. Coulomb went all along the compound on the side of the swimming-bath to the end of the pasture, returning in a straight line back to Colonel's bungalow up to the terrace, where it was lifted up and lowered down to give it a vapoury appearance" (quoted in Caldwell, *A Casebook of Encounters*, Case 34).

In her own defense, Blavatsky wrote:

Mr. A. O. Hume, of Simla, received letters in his own library when alone from the Mahatmas, in answer to letters just written, and when I was at Bombay. The handwriting was the same; evidently there must be forgers about—writing in the Mahatma's writing and on his special paper—besides me. You cannot say I write the answers. The Coulombs have left, but still there are replies. Are we all a pack of self-deceived idiots, or fraudulent impostors? If the latter, what object can we have? We make no money. We seek no notoriety. We only gain abuse. What do we gain? (CW 6:312)

Blavatsky and Olcott were in Paris when they learned of Emma's vow of revenge, and Olcott wrote to Madame Coulomb, saying: "My information is that you are talking about your having lent H.P.B. money in Egypt, which has not been refunded; that Mon. Coulomb has made trap-doors and other apparatus for trick manifestations by her; that you have various secrets about her that you might reveal; and that you openly express your hostility to the Theosophical Society" (Gomes, *The Coulomb Case*). The "trick manifestations" were letters supposedly coming from the Masters.

H.P.B. also wrote to Emma telling her that she could never ruin the Society, but only ruin H.P.B. in the estimation of her friends. The Coulombs responded to protest their innocence and asked whether Alexis could still be in charge of H.P.B.'s rooms. In spite of their protests, the General Council of the Society voted to expel the Coulombs from Adyar. They refused to leave but finally were forced to go.

At the time, the Christian missionaries in India were the sworn enemies of the Theosophical Society, and Blavatsky in particular, because they saw H.P.B. and the Society as a threat to Christianity. Madame Coulomb knew she would find a welcome hearing with the missionaries, so she headed straight for them after leaving Adyar. She told the missionaries in Madras that, when she knew Blavatsky in Cairo, Blavatsky was a woman of low morals. Yet in 1879, five years before the charge of forgery and fraud, she had defended Madame Blavatsky against an attack by writing a letter to the Anglo-Indian Ceylon *Times* of June 5, saying:

> I have known [Madame Blavatsky] for these last eight years, and I must say the truth, that there is nothing against her character. We lived in the same town, and on the contrary she was considered one of the cleverest ladies of the age. Madame B. is a musician, a painter, a linguist, an author, and I may say that very few ladies and indeed few gentlemen have a knowledge of things in general as Madame Blavatsky. (Quoted in Cranston, *H.P.B.*, p. 245)

If nothing else, Madame Coulomb was quite capable of spinning a story any way she wished for personal gain.

The most disastrous and upsetting charge of forgery and fraud came to be known as "the Hodgson Report." In November 1884, Dr. Richard Hodgson of the Society for Psychical Research (SPR) went to Adyar to investigate the charges of fraud that the Coulombs had alleged. After examining what evidence he could find, he concluded that the Mahatma Letters were written and sent by Blavatsky. He agreed with the Coulombs that Koot Hoomi was a fictitious character and that the supposed astral visions of him were produced by the Coulombs or other confederates of H.P.B. All of it was put down to ingenious trickery.

In April 1986, about a hundred years after the SPR published the Hodgson Report, Dr. Vernon Harrison of the same society published a critical analysis of the original Hodgson Report. He found that it was "riddled with slanted statements, conjectures advanced as fact or probably fact, uncorroborated testimony of unnamed witnesses, selection of evidence and downright falsity" (Harrison, *H. P. Blavatsky*). Just as the British Museum handwriting experts had said when they accepted the Mahatma Letters, Harrison concluded that the letters could not have been written by Blavatsky. Since Harrison was a member of the SPR, but not of the Theosophical Society, and since he was a past president of the Royal Photographic Society and research manager to De La Rue firm, printers of banknotes, passports, and the like, he probably knew as much about forgery as anyone living.

Unfortunately, there is no way to go back to evidence long gone and prove that the Mahatma Letters were written by adepts and that the claimed sightings of Masters by at least twenty-five reputable people were true. We can, however, reliably accept the testimony of experts that the Mahatma Letters were not written by Blavatsky. The whole affair caused H.P.B. tremendous psychological pain. She wanted to sue the Coulombs, but Olcott and others strongly advised her not to do so because it would drag the names of the Masters into court, and the Masters would not appear in court to defend themselves or Blavatsky.

In addition to improvable charges of forgery and fraud, a serious charge of plagiarism was leveled against K.H. in the early 1800s. The charge and the subsequent uproar among the British came to be known as "the Kiddle incident." K.H. had given Sinnett permission to quote anything from his letters that he thought might be useful. With that permission in mind, Sinnett used some quotations from K.H.'s letters in his book, *The Occult World*, published in 1881. He included one that read, "Plato was right: *ideas* rule the world" (ML, letter 12, p. 39).

Unknown to both Sinnett and K.H., an American spiritualist by the name of Henry Kiddle had used that passage in a talk he had given at Lake Pleasant, New York. When Kiddle read the passage in Sinnett's book, he was shocked to find that his words were used verbatim and without his permission and without credit to himself. Apparently when K.H. used the same words that Kiddle had, he used them to illustrate a very different point. That further upset Kiddle, who accused K.H. of distorting the ideas K.H. had borrowed "to suit his own very different purpose." Kiddle complained of the "theft" in a letter to Stainton Moses, editor of an English spiritualist journal, and Moses published the letter in the September 1, 1883, issue of his journal. A great deal of correspondence went back and forth over the alleged plagiarism, and it left Sinnett so upset over what he called the "wretched little Kiddle incident" that he mentioned it in a letter to K.H. K.H. did not address the issue for some time because he thought it rather unimportant. When he realized how much it upset Sinnett, however, he decided to explain how the "plagiarism" had occurred. K.H. said that the solution to the problem was simple, and so amusing that were it not for the pain it caused some of his true friends, he would still be laughing at it. K.H. explained:

> The letter in question was framed by me while on a journey and on horse-back. It was dictated mentally, in the direction of, and "precipitated" by, a young chela not yet expert at this branch of psychic chemistry, and who had to transcribe it from the hardly visible imprint. Half of it, therefore, was omitted and the other half more or less distorted by the "artist." When asked by him at the time, whether I would look it over and correct I answered, imprudently I confess—"anyhow will do, my boy—it is of no great importance if you skip a few words." I was physically very tired by a ride of 48 hours consecutively, and (physically again)—half asleep. Besides this I had very important business to attend to *psychically* and therefore little remained of me to devote to that letter. It was doomed, I suppose. When I woke I found it had already been sent on, and, as I was not then anticipating its publication, I never gave it from that time a thought. (ML, letter 117, p. 398)

In further explanation of the "plagiarized" passage, K.H. says that when using "mental telegraphy" to transmit a letter to a chela, two things are necessary. First, the sender must clearly concentrate on what he wants to transmit; and second, the receiver must be completely passive. Any disturbance on either end would result in imperfection. If thought wanders, the connection is broken and the result is confusing.

K.H. said that when transmitting the letter, he had a "psychic diagnosis of current Spiritualistic thought" in mind and saw the Lake Pleasant speech as a good example. Therefore, he transmitted that idea more vividly than his own remarks and conclusions on the subject. That caused the remarks from Mr. Kiddle to come out more brightly than his own remarks that were "hardly visible and quite blurred" on the paper. In further explanation of the problem, K.H. explains:

> I never forget what I once see or read. A bad habit. So much so, that often and unconsciously to myself I string together sentences of stray words and phrases before my eyes, and which may have been used a hundred years ago or will be a hundred years hence, in relation to quite a different subject. Laziness and real lack of time. The "Old Lady" called me a "brain pirate" and a plagiarist the other day for using a whole sentence of five lines which, she is firmly convinced, I must have pilfered from Dr. Wilder's brain, as three months later he reproduced it in an essay of his on prophetic intuition. Never had a look into the old philosopher's brain cells. Got it somewhere in a northern current—don't know. (ML, letter 20, p. 75)

We must not judge Kiddle too harshly for accusing K.H. of plagiarism. The words used did come from Kiddle, and K.H.

had used them without permission and as though they were his own words. In the eyes of K.H., there was no such thing as plagiarism. Ideas could not be copyrighted and by using words best expressing ideas it did not matter who had first said them. To the Westerner, however, plagiarism is a crime. Hence the two disparate views clashed and the problem arose.

PART II

THE PATH

Chapter 13

THERE IS A ROAD

Throughout the spiritual literature of the world, a road, a path, or a journey has been used as a metaphor for a way of life that leads to enlightenment or heaven. It is always a road that is fraught with difficulties and dangers to life itself, and few there be who choose to travel it. Theosophical philosophy asserts that the spiritual road is such a road. It is a steep road with dangers lurking at every turn, yet it is a road that can be traveled by the brave and the pure of heart.

After the death of H. P. Blavatsky, a short document known as "There Is a Road" was found among her papers. It beautifully and succinctly describes the road to enlightenment. It reads:

There is a road, steep and thorny, beset with perils of every kind, but yet a road, and it leads to the very heart of the universe. I can tell you how to find those who will show you the secret gateway that opens inward only and closes fast behind

the neophyte for evermore. There is no danger that dauntless courage cannot conquer. There is no trial that spotless
purity cannot pass through. There is no difficulty that strong
intellect cannot surmount. For those who win onward, there
is reward past all telling, the power to bless and save humanity. For those who fail, there are other lives in which success
may come.

Blavatsky was neither a doomsday prophet nor a Pollyanna.
She told it like it is. The road to enlightenment is filled with
dangers and hardships, yet it is passable if we possess the necessary qualifications.

The less traveled road is often spoken of in legends and in poetry. In 1920, Robert Frost wrote "The Road Not Taken." That
poem ends: "Two roads diverged in a wood, and I—/ I took the
one less traveled by, / And that has made all the difference."

Plato describes the road in his cave analogy. All the residents
of the allegorical cave are chained to their seats. They can only
look straight ahead to the wall on which shadows are moving.
That wall and its shadows are the real world to them. They know
of no other. One day one of the chained men frees himself from
the chains and turns to face the opposite direction. He finds a
ray of light coming in toward the wall and he follows it to its
source. The trail is exceedingly difficult to follow. There are
sharp rocks and many obstacles in his way, yet he presses on in
spite of the fact that his body is bloody from scratches and falls
along the way. At last he reaches the surface and is blinded by the
sun, and he realizes that it is the sun that has been causing the

shadows on the cave wall. Eventually his eyes adjust and he realizes that this is the true light, the true world, and that everything that he and the others have believed to be the real world is but shadows. He has been liberated. He is free of the terrible delusion, and he returns to the cave to tell the others that he has found reality. As might be expected, no one believes him.

We are the people in Plato's cave. It is we who see the shadows of reality and judge them to be the real world. As K.H. pointed out to Sinnett, we judge by appearances, but the Masters never do. Those who are brave enough to go through the secret gateway enter upon the road to the ultimate source of all, to the real word, the unchanging, the Eternal. The cave analogy is Plato's version of "There Is a Road." In Christianity, that road is known as "The Way of the Cross"; in Judaism, "The Way of Holiness"; in Buddhism, "The Noble Eightfold Path"; and no doubt it is known by other names in other traditions, as well as in legends in which the hero must go through terrible trials to get to his goal.

As psychologist Carl Jung pointed out, we all have a shadow side, but we are often unable or unwilling to admit that we have a shadow side at all. Nevertheless, our subconscious may reveal our faults to us in dreams in which we make someone else the guilty party. To get at those faults and to conquer them, we must pass through the "secret gateway that opens inwardly only." It opens inwardly to everything in our nature. The road opens up to our faults, our strengths, our hopes and desires. Much further along the way, that road leads to the inner self that is rooted in "the heart of the universe." If that gateway opened only to our self-image, it would not close forevermore because we can revise our self-image. We can begin life as a Jew, a Christian, or a Hindu and later convert to another religion or become a Theosophist or an atheist. To travel the road beyond the open gateway, we will have to have a never-failing will to press on and be willing to sacrifice personal wants for the greater good.

The road beyond the secret gateway leads toward self-knowledge. At the beginning of our journey we are easily self-deceived. We discover an aspect of our nature that was previously unknown to us, and we say, "This is I. This is the Self." Be fore-warned. So long as there is an "I" that claims to be the Self, we are deceived. It can be put no more beautifully than in *The Voice of the Silence* (verse 1): "When waxing stronger, thy Soul glides forth from her secure retreat: and breaking loose from the pro-tecting shrine, extends her silver thread and rushes onward; when beholding her image on the waves of Space she whispers, 'This is I,'—declare, O Disciple, that thy soul is caught in the webs of delusion." When that Self is realized, there is no duality. There is no one to say: "This is I." There is only Eternity.

The "perils of every kind" are perils within our own nature. Every transition stage in us is associated with some danger: childbirth, puberty, marriage, and a myriad other transitions we encounter throughout life. On the way, we discover how difficult it is to let go of the little self with which we have identified for so long. Yet to reach the goal, *everything personal* must be aban-doned. Whether or not one takes the crucifixion story of Jesus to be history or myth, at the end Jesus is left utterly alone and is even stripped of his garments. His agony may symbolize for us what St. John of the Cross called "the dark night of the soul." We go through many of these dark nights during life, but darkest of all is the one before the dawn of enlightenment. St. John of the Cross seems to have been aware of this when he said that the soul is closest to God when it believes itself to be farthest away from God.

We pass through the secret gateway with theories about the inner self, about the spiritual nature, and about the divine. Yet until we experience that totally new state of consciousness called the "inner self," we have only theories. The truth remains secret to us. Once we experience the inner self, it can never be forgotten. The gateway closes fast behind us forevermore.

To travel the road to its end, we need courage, purity, strong intellect, and more. To enter the path, we must be determined to search for truth, no matter what that truth may be. The search begins long before we realize what that search will entail. It begins with a search for meaning.

Chapter 14

THE SEARCH
FOR MEANING

One of the most powerful drives in human beings is the drive to find meaning. We need to have some explanation for almost everything. If we hear a loud, unfamiliar noise in the night, the first thing we do is ask, "What was that?" We may decide that the noise came from something falling in the kitchen, and that may satisfy us. Or we may be completely perplexed by the sound. In that case, we are likely to search for the source of the noise. Unless we decide that the disturbance is harmless, we feel compelled to find out what caused the crash. We may conclude that the noise is from a falling pot we left poorly balanced on a countertop, and we may be right. We may be wrong, however. No matter whether we are right or wrong, once we have assigned meaning to the unfamiliar sound we will probably relax.

When a very young child asks, "Where did I come from?" that child may be asking a far more profound question than the one the parents imagine. Rather than asking a question about the origin of the body, the child may really be asking, "Where did I come from?" Dawning within the child there may be a dim realization of the true self and at the same time an inability to pinpoint its origin. The child has begun to search for meaning.

As we grow older, most of us drop the search for meaning. We are busy with growing up, discovering the world and our place in it, finding a career, and looking for a mate. It is often not until after we are settled into middle age that the question arises again. We may then ask that question of ourselves and this time add two more: "What is my destiny?" and "Is there any purpose to life?" No matter what our preconceived ideas about who and what we are, those questions reveal that we are searching for the origin of our own consciousness. If we are convinced materialists, we will most likely begin with a genealogical search. We will seek answers to such questions as "Who are my ancestors? Were they all born here or did they emigrate from elsewhere?" and "What did they do for a living?" We may answer the questions "Where did I (the body) come from?" and "What is my destiny (death)?" But we have not answered the question about purpose. We have not answered the "why" of life. If we are materialists, we may be convinced that there is no purpose to life, and hence it is a waste of time to attempt to find one.

Religious people may seek answers to the question about purpose in religious doctrine. People who regard themselves as spiritual, but not necessarily religious, may seek answers elsewhere. Perhaps they will begin by comparing various religious and philosophical teachings. By doing so, they may discover a wisdom tradition that runs through all religions. They may discover that a central teaching of that tradition is that the answers to ultimate questions lie within our own consciousness and that thousands have had flashes of insight into the same universal truths. Even in exoteric Christian scriptures, we may find phrases suggesting the possibility that truth lies within. St. Paul speaks of "Christ in you, the hope of glory," and the Christ claims that he is the way, the truth, and the life. He also taught that the kingdom of heaven is within. Other religions have expressed similar ideas in their own way and clothed them in the language of their own culture.

For years, Albert Schweitzer wondered if he could discover a universal concept of the ethical. No doubt he put a great deal of effort into his studies, and no doubt he spent many a day and night pondering that profound question. It has been reported that one day while peacefully floating down the Nile on a barge, he realized the answer: reverence for life. More than likely, that flash of understanding was a flash of insight from the universal state of consciousness called "buddhi." Flashes of understanding such as that always come when the mind is still. A great deal of thought precedes the insight, but only when the mind becomes quiet is it possible to get such a powerful insight.

The Dalai Lama has noted that all of the great religious traditions have one thing in common: compassion. It takes but a little thought to realize that reverence for life and compassion are inseparably linked. The fact that there are fundamentally similar codes of ethics among the world's religions and philosophies poses an important question. Why are reverence for life and compassion almost universally acknowledged as the basis for right behavior?

In one of the few instances that the Masters spoke of extraterrestrial beings, they said that what they call "planetary spirits" exist, beings who are neither angels nor gods but rather are best thought of as intelligent powers of nature. Those beings, said the Masters:

> appear on Earth but at the origin of every *new* human kind [and] they remain with man no longer than the time required for the eternal truths they teach to impress themselves so forcibly upon the plastic minds of the new races as to warrant them from being lost or entirely forgotten in ages hereafter, by the forthcoming generations. The mission of the planetary Spirit is but to strike the KEY NOTE OF TRUTH. Once he has directed the vibration of the latter to run its course uninterruptedly along the catenation of that race and to the end of the cycle—the denizen of the highest inhabited sphere disappears from the surface of our planet—till the following "resurrection of flesh." The vibrations of the Primitive Truth are what your philosophers name "innate ideas." (ML, letter 18, pp. 59–60)

If what the Master says is true, that would explain the commonality of such nearly universally accepted virtues as compassion and reverence for life. Of course, different societies apply those virtues differently, and they do not always apply them to all. The Jains, for example, wear masks to keep them from accidently killing an insect that might fly into their mouth or nose. Some societies teach that it is proper to raise, kill, and eat animals. Others preach vegetarianism. Capital punishment, abortion, and other examples might be cited to show how these universal concepts of the ethical are applied or not applied.

The Theosophical Society has no list of commandments. Members are free to decide for themselves what is ethical. Nevertheless, Theosophical literature offers very definite guidelines to the ethical life, and it links living an ethical life to an essential step on the path to adeptship. In a letter to the fourth annual American convention of the Theosophical Society, Blavatsky wrote:

> the Ethics of Theosophy are more important than any divulgement of psychic laws and facts. The latter relate wholly to the material and evanescent part of the septenary man, but the Ethics sink into and take hold of the real man—the reincarnating Ego. We are outwardly creatures of but a day; within we are eternal. Learn, then, well the doctrines of Karma and Reincarnation, and teach, practice, promulgate that system of life and thought which alone can save the coming races. Do not work merely for the Theosophical Society, but through it for Humanity. (CW 12:156)

Blavatsky said that *The Secret Doctrine* was written to appeal to the "higher faculties." It was not written simply to present another theory about cosmogenesis and anthropogenesis. Rather, it was meant to stimulate insight into essential truths; and at least theoretically, when those truths are realized, they result in an experience of the ultimate unity of all, and that experience of unity results in a life of altruism and compassion for all. H.P.B. gave a hint of that early on in *The Secret Doctrine*, where she wrote: "Lead the life necessary . . . and Wisdom will come to you naturally" (SD 1:167). Blavatsky's statement leaves us wondering what that necessary life might be and how living it might bring wisdom to us naturally. Fortunately, she has given us a short piece that outlines some essential features of that life. The document is called "The Golden Stairs."

Chapter 15

THE GOLDEN STAIRS

Blavatsky tells us that one of the Masters, probably Morya, gave her a brief summary of the requirements that lead to what he called "The Temple of Divine Wisdom," and he told her to give it to those who had volunteered to be taught by her. Most likely it was meant for her students in the Esoteric School, but everyone who aspires to live the spiritual life can benefit from it. The document is short, but there are many levels of meaning in it. It is called "The Golden Stairs."

> Behold the truth before you: a clean life, an open mind, a pure heart, an eager intellect, an unveiled spiritual perception, a brotherliness for one's co-disciple, a readiness to give and receive advice and instruction, a loyal sense of duty to the Teacher, a willing obedience to the behests of TRUTH, once we have placed our confidence in, and believe that Teacher to

be in possession of it; a courageous endurance of personal injustice, a brave declaration of principles, a valiant defense of those who are unjustly attacked, and a constant eye to the ideal of human progression and perfection which the secret science (Gupta-Vidya) depicts—these are the golden stairs up the steps of which the learner may climb to the Temple of Divine Wisdom. (CW 12:591)

If we want to probe the meaning of each step, it makes sense to start at the beginning. The stairs must be lived sequentially, but paradoxically all of the stairs must be lived simultaneously. For example, what would be the motivation to live a clean life if we did not believe that humans could make progress? And must we have an eager intellect before we are willing to defend those who are unjustly attacked? Taking the stairs sequentially, we might ponder each in turn.

A CLEAN LIFE

Every religion teaches that we are meant to live an ethical life. True, the ethics are not always identical in the way we are taught to apply them, but all major traditions have very similar ideas about the right way to treat our fellow human beings. No matter our religion or the lack thereof, we are taught not to kill others needlessly. We are taught not to steal, and on the positive side we are taught to help the poor and to love our neighbor as ourself.

The essence of a clean life is almost identical in every culture, but is "a clean life" in "The Golden Stairs" more than that? Isn't it possible to keep all the commandments, to help the poor, and even to shun the cardinal sin of pride while having a mind that is filthy and emotions that are gross? To live a clean life means that every aspect of our nature must be clean. Without that total cleanliness, all the other requirements become more difficult, if not impossible, to perfect.

AN OPEN MIND

Most people would probably define an open mind as one that is open to points of view other than its own. Those with an open mind are able to understand different theories and beliefs, but that does not necessarily cause them to change their own view in favor of another one. Open-minded people are not those who are so easily influenced that they can be swayed by whoever is speaking loudest. In fact, they may hold some very strong beliefs, especially political and religious ones.

While some religions encourage a completely open mind, others do not, at least not when it comes to religious doctrine. In Christianity, one must accept an authorized creed to join a church. In contrast to that, Jews are more apt to accept a common practice rather than a common set of beliefs. Atheists and those who are not religiously observant may or may not hold intransigent positions on everything from politics to religion.

Those who hold intransigent positions have ideas set in proverbial stone, and facts will not confuse them.

In a university study entitled, "How Facts Backfire," political partisans were given what appeared to be newspaper articles about current affairs. Each article contained some widely held beliefs that were provably false. One would expect that when the false information was corrected, people would accept the facts even if they did not like them. That did not happen. Instead, the researchers discovered that when supplied with the truth, the political conservatives in the study actually became more firmly convinced that their own point of view was correct. Political liberals did not do that, but they did conveniently forget or ignore facts that did not conform to their beliefs. Neither the conservatives nor the liberals in the study had open minds. What few realize is that, when we are truly open-minded, we are willing to drop *our own* most precious belief in the face of evidence that proves it wrong. Neither this step nor any of the others of "The Golden Stairs" is an easy one to climb.

A PURE HEART

All words are ambiguous and over time are likely to change their meanings. Neither do we all understand the same meaning in any given word. In common speech today, most people define *heart* as the physical organ. They might also interpret it as referring to emotions. Those who say they are heart people rather than head people probably mean they operate more from the way they feel emotionally than from the way their intellect might direct. Few would define *heart* as the "seat of wisdom," yet that is the way a Buddhist might define it. It is the latter definition that comes closest to a Theosophical view.

Wisdom, like compassion, is impersonal. When we act with wisdom, our motives are pure. We have no ulterior personal motives. We do what we do because it is the right thing to do, not because we see some personal benefit in our actions. The Christian mystic Meister Eckhart once said that people do not love God rightly if they love him for some purpose. To tread the spiritual path, we must have a pure heart, one that is free from selfish motives. The heart of compassionate action is described beautifully in *The Voice of the Silence* (verses 59–62):

Let thy Soul lend its ear to every cry of pain like as the lotus bares its heart to drink the morning sun. Let not the fierce Sun dry one tear of pain before thyself hast wiped it from the sufferer's eye. But let each burning human tear drop on thy heart and there remain, nor ever brush it off, until the pain that caused it is removed. These tears, O thou of heart most merciful, these are the streams that irrigate the fields of charity immortal. 'Tis on such soil that grows the midnight blossom of Buddha more difficult to find, more rare to view than is the flower of the Vogay tree.

AN EAGER INTELLECT

It is not enough to have a mind that is open to new ideas. That is a passive, not an active, state. One must be possessed of an intellect that actively pursues truth. The October 1887 issue of Blavatsky's magazine *Lucifer* includes a short article titled "Self-Knowledge," which she presumably wrote. The article points out that more than intellect is required. We must first acknowledge that we are ignorant of our true nature. Then we must be convinced that we can discover self-knowledge. If we are convinced that we cannot know something, we will never try to find out, so the second requirement is to be convinced that we can reach our goal. Blavatsky agrees with what the ancient Greeks taught: "Man, know thyself," and she believes we can do just that. The article reads:

> The first necessity for obtaining self-knowledge is to become profoundly conscious of ignorance; to feel with every fibre of the heart that one is *ceaselessly* self-deceived. The second requisite is the still deeper conviction that such knowledge— such intuitive and certain knowledge—can be obtained by effort. The third and most important is an indomitable determination to obtain and face that knowledge. Self-knowledge of this kind is unattainable by what men usually call "self-analysis." It is not reached by reasoning or any brain process; for it is the awakening to consciousness of the Divine

nature of man. To obtain this knowledge is a greater achievement than to command the elements or to know the future. (Reprinted in CW 8:108)

AN UNVEILED
SPIRITUAL PERCEPTION

We perceive the physical world through our five senses, but we cannot perceive the spiritual world through physical senses. This step on the stairs requires that we become aware of a deeper state of reality that we often call "spiritual." When we look into the eyes of a fellow human being and realize that the conscious life in them is the same as the conscious life in us, we have for that moment become one with them. That is spiritual perception, but at that stage it is not yet fully unveiled. Gradually we can become aware that all creatures, including animals, trees, and plants, are conscious and that the life in them is the same as the life in us. Eventually it becomes possible to perceive that unity even in strangers and, yes, even in enemies.

A Sufi exercise can help us to realize unity with others, even with people we do not like. A group of people form two circles, an inside circle and an outside circle. Each person on the inside circle faces a person on the outside circle. Each pair around the two circles is asked to walk around each other and look directly into the eyes of the other person. Neither person is to show any facial expression, nor are they to say a word to each other. While circling each other, each is to think: "I see the God in you. You see the God in me." After circling each other three times, holding that intent, the outer circle moves clockwise to the next person, the inner circle moves counterclockwise to the next person, and the exercise is repeated. When the group is large, it will almost certainly include some individuals that each person is fond of and some who may even be perceived of as "difficult" people. If the exercise is done with an open mind and with a sincere attempt to see the divinity in the other person, there is a chance that one will actually, for a moment at least, perceive unity.

Annie Besant once said that love is the response to a realization of oneness. If we reflect on that, we will probably realize that when we feel a rush of affection for a person or an animal, we have for a moment been at one with them. There was no sense of a separate *me* at the moment the love rushes out from us. It may be that when we become aware of the ultimate unity of all, compassion pours out from us. The word *love* tends to be used more for personal affection, whereas the word *compassion* tends to be impersonal, universal love. No definition of those two words can adequately describe the experience of them, but those who have had the experience no longer believe. They know.

A BROTHERLINESS FOR ONE'S CO-DISCIPLE

Although originally the term *co-disciple* was almost certainly meant for members of the ES, it applies to everyone, because in one sense everyone is our co-disciple in life. All men are our brothers and all women our sisters. In the phrase "an unveiled spiritual perception," the word *perception* is a noun and as such it is static. Brotherliness for one's co-disciple implies action. Once we recognize a fundamental unity among our co-disciples, action follows. The realization of unity compels us to act as brothers and sisters, to care for one another, to be there for one another.

A READINESS TO GIVE AND RECEIVE ADVICE AND INSTRUCTION

We can always find those who know more than we do, and we can find those who know less than we do. Although people may know that, some find it very difficult to take advice and instruction, and some find it very difficult to give advice and instruction. Perhaps what makes it difficult for some is that they misunderstand what this step is asking us to do. To give and receive advice and instruction does not mean that we are to tell others what they should do because we believe we know best. Likewise, it does not mean that we should do what others tell us to do because we think *they* know best.

When a friend comes to us for help with a personal problem, the best thing we can do to help them is to give them no advice at all. If we are aware of the spiritual nature and we have a brotherliness for our co-disciple, we can simply listen to our friend with the intent of being in rapport with them spiritually. Then it is possible that we will get an insight into what to say to our friend.

Rather than telling them what we think they should do, we can simply point out various options that occur to us and ask them to consider all options. It is similar to shining a flashlight in dark corners and saying, "Do you see anything there that might help you?" The decision about what to do or not to do should be left entirely to the friend.

The Masters make it clear that they don't tell even their most advanced students what they should do in personal matters. Blavatsky often said that she was "ordered" to do something, but the orders given to her were similar to what a supervisor might tell an employee to do. The employee has agreed to follow the supervisor's directions; but at any time, the employee is free to resign and seek employment elsewhere. Students of the Masters are equally free to resign. *The Voice of the Silence* tells us that the Teacher can but point the way, and Plato tells us that the true teacher is a midwife. If we try to tell others what to do, we are likely to cause our friend to have a metaphorical miscarriage. More than that, if our friend does what we tell them to do, the karma of their action will rebound more on us than on them.

A LOYAL SENSE OF DUTY
TO THE TEACHER

Who is the Teacher? The Teacher might be a guru, a Master, or perhaps the Teacher is our own inner self. Gurus and Masters can inform us of facts, but no one can give us understanding.

Understanding always comes from within. Therefore, it would seem that the only true Teacher is our inner self. All other teachers are, as Plato pointed out, midwives.

A WILLING OBEDIENCE TO THE BEHESTS OF TRUTH

Since all words are ambiguous, we risk misunderstanding if we do not define our terms. The word *truth* has been used in several ways. It may refer to facts, but it may also refer to principles or what has sometimes been called "eternal verities." This step on "The Golden Stairs" refers to principles, not to facts. Specifically, it asks that we act on insights into truth. It is important to distinguish between our beliefs and insight.

We fill our minds with opinions and beliefs about nearly everything. Frequently, we hold very strong views about religion. Without proof, we may be convinced there is a God, especially the one we have created in our own minds. Usually that God is rather like us, except that He (masculine, of course) is omniscient and omnipotent. Voltaire once said something to the effect that God created man in his own image, and we have been repaying the compliment ever since. Frequently, atheists and agnostics hold to their unproven beliefs just as strongly as the theists hold to theirs. Perhaps our beliefs have been formed on the basis of some evidence, but none of our beliefs have come to us as insights. When we get an insight into truth, it comes as a flash of understanding that destroys our previously held belief. When that flash radiates through our mind, we experience a deep joy. We feel integrated and peaceful. Our beliefs and opinions never have that effect on us. When someone challenges our beliefs, we may become stubbornly defensive and even respond in anger. Perhaps our point of view is correct; perhaps it is not. We form our beliefs out of our conditioned mind and out of what evidence we can muster to prove our belief. We cannot form an insight into truth. The latter comes from beyond our conditioned mind and replaces a belief with an unimpeachable truth.

As we begin to lead the necessary life, flashes of insight will come to us more frequently, but only if we act on the knowledge that has been reflected in our mind. We must have a "willing obedience to the behests of truth," not only a passive recognition of truth. We must have confidence in the Teacher, the source of insights. If we hold our beliefs as theories rather than intransigent positions, we will be able to drop them when insight reveals that our beliefs are either false or incomplete.

A COURAGEOUS ENDURANCE OF PERSONAL INJUSTICE

A courageous endurance of personal injustice does not mean that we should refuse to defend ourselves from abuse. What it does mean is that we should not react to personal injustice by getting angry, depressed, or fearful. Insofar as we can, we have a right to defend ourselves. Once we have done all we can, this step requires us to endure, without emotional upset, what we cannot change. To do that requires an enormous amount of self-control. Most of us fail this step more often than we succeed. If it is any comfort, Blavatsky had an especially hard time with this one. When she was unjustly accused of writing the Mahatma Letters, she became so upset that the Masters said they could not use her for weeks. Nevertheless, we cannot use Blavatsky's failure to justify our own failure. As the Masters have repeatedly said, we must *try*.

A BRAVE DECLARATION
OF PRINCIPLES

Frequently, we do not say or do what we know to be right because we fear negative personal consequences. One of the Upanishads has summed up this problem rather well. It reads: "The sweet is one thing. The right is another." In the ancient world, Socrates made a brave declaration of principles and suffered a courageous endurance of the injustice that followed. He had a chance to escape from execution when his disciples offered to bribe the jailers, but Socrates declined. His disciples could not understand it. They reasoned that all he had to do was to leave Athens. Instead, Socrates stood his ground. He said he would not renounce his principles nor would he teach others to disobey the law by bribing the guards so that he could escape from prison. Claiming that he was not afraid of death, he drank the hemlock. Today, the world knows about Socrates, but few know anything about his accusers.

A more modern example is that of Annie Besant, second international president of the Theosophical Society. She worked closely with Mohandas Gandhi to help free India from colonial rule and enjoyed enormous popularity and praise from the Indian people. At one point during her work with Gandhi, she disagreed with him. Gandhi did not want one British soldier to remain in India, whereas Besant believed that if the British forces were to be totally removed, there would be a bloodbath in India. Although she knew full well that parting with Gandhi would make her lose her popularity with the people, she stood by her principles and accepted the consequences. Whether or not she was right is not the point. The point is that she did not shrink from stating her principles merely because it would make her unpopular.

A VALIANT DEFENSE OF THOSE WHO ARE UNJUSTLY ATTACKED

The operative word on this step of "The Golden Stairs" is *defense*. Often we are tempted to respond to injustice with an attack on the perpetrator. Strong action may be required in some cases, but we must never allow our defense of a victim to become aggression against the perpetrator. This step is related to the previous two. In defending someone against an unjust attack, we are declaring a principle, but we must do so without regard to the personal injustice the defense may elicit. Often our defense will prompt a new attack, this time on us. The requirement is "a valiant defense," and that means we must be brave enough to defend those who are unjustly attacked even if we know that we will be attacked for our defense.

A CONSTANT EYE TO THE IDEAL OF HUMAN PROGRESSION AND PERFECTION THAT THE SECRET SCIENCE DEPICTS

We must keep this step in mind from the very beginning of our journey. If we were not convinced that the human race could progress spiritually and ultimately develop human potential to its limit, we would have little interest in trying to climb the Golden Stairs. In this step, the word *perfection* means "complete." The biblical command "Be ye perfect" is often taken as an impossible, even absurd, order. That would be true if we took *perfect* to mean "without even the slightest flaw or error." The physical world is only an approximation of an ideal world. We might call to mind that there is no such thing as a perfectly straight line in the physical world. All straight lines are approximations of the ideal straight line. The same can be said for a point. Points have no dimension whatsoever. Dots merely represent points. Keeping this in mind, human perfection, meaning fully developed potential, becomes reasonable and achievable.

These are the Golden Stairs up which the learner may climb to the Temple of Divine Wisdom: the Temple of Divine Wisdom is a metaphor for the inner self. Our task is to learn to focus our consciousness in the heart, the seat of wisdom according to the Buddhists, or buddhi-manas according to Theosophy. Most of the time, we identify with the *me* or kama-manas. That state of consciousness is centered in the solar plexus. We might get some sense of that physical centering when we realize that emotional trauma often upsets our stomach. It is of little use to remain identified with the *me* and from there try to raise our consciousness to a spiritual state. By living an altruistic life, by climbing the Golden Stairs, we are more and more functioning from that deeper state of consciousness known as the "inner self." As H.P.B. has told us, if we live the necessary life, wisdom will come to us naturally. It is impossible to force it by personal desire or by imagining ourselves to be functioning from a spiritual state of consciousness. Desire and even pity come from the *me*, but it is only from the inner self that compassion can become a realized, beneficent power.

Chapter 16

PITFALLS ON THE PATH

W e would like to follow the Golden Stairs, but faced with the difficult task of doing so, we give up. G. K. Chesterton once said that Christianity was not tried and found hard. It was found hard and not tried. We might say the same about the Golden Stairs.

The Gospel according to St. Matthew (26:41) tells us: "Watch and pray, that ye enter not into temptation: the spirit indeed is willing, but the flesh is weak." Why is it frequently so difficult to carry out our good intentions? We resolve to overcome a bad habit, but often it requires so much energy and patience that we give up. New Year's resolutions are broken more often than they are fulfilled.

The body, emotions, and mind are conditioned by repetitive action. It is not so difficult to become aware of physical habits. Compared to emotional and mental habits, physical habits such as smoking are relatively easy to overcome. Habits are formed by repetitive action. Like water seeking the route of least resistance, our emotional and mental energy does the same. We react in a certain way to a particular situation, and when confronted by the same circumstances again, we tend to repeat the reaction. It becomes embedded in the subconscious. We react automatically without any thought at all. Then we tend to say to ourselves and our friends, "That's how I am. It is my nature." Of course it is not our nature. It is a mental-emotional habit pattern that we have created and that we can change.

Inertia operates not only at the physical level. There is emotional, mental, and even spiritual inertia. The well-known dictum of Newton states that a body at rest tends to remain at rest, and a body in motion tends to remain in motion unless the body is acted upon by an outside force. Our emotional and mental habits are subject to inertia, and the more we repeat them, the more we reinforce their strength and the harder it is to change them. We may notice emotional inertia when we come home from a late-night party and realize that we cannot go to sleep until we calm down. Our emotions are racing with the excitement we experienced at the party. Only when the emotions "are acted upon by an outside force," our mind and will, or for lack of new excitement they exhaust themselves, are we able to sleep.

It is more difficult to become aware of mental inertia. We form opinions about people and reinforce them every time we meet them. We choose political sides and tend to ignore negative information about our candidate and positive information about our opponent. We do the same with religion and countless other subjects. It may be that we are good examples of a case put forward by Jiddu Krishnamurti when he allegedly said that "the only difference between an insane person and a sane person is that an insane person has one fixed idea and a sane person has many fixed ideas." Some of us set our ideas in stone and find it difficult if not impossible to see a different point of view. According to some psychologists, those who cannot see the alternate image in an optical illusion are also those who find it difficult to see another point of view. If accurate, that would be a way we might ascertain whether or not we tend to hold intransigent positions.

Politically, culturally, and socially, mental inertia becomes obvious. Every pioneer who tries to go against strong public opinion will almost certainly be attacked, jailed, or even murdered for holding a view that is contrary to the accepted view.

Strong opinions and fixed beliefs are a greater block than alcoholic beverages. The latter are harmful, but erroneous beliefs are more harmful. Unfortunately, we are often unaware that our opinions are just that—opinions—rather than uncontestable facts. We are apt to judge people on slim evidence, or on one or two incidents. K.H. warned Sinnett that he was becoming dogmatic and that if he persisted in his tendency to dogmatism and unjust misconceptions of persons and motives, it would forever end all correspondence from him.

We must not be too hard on Sinnett, because we are all products of our time and our cultural conditioning. The British who ruled India in the 1880s tended to think of the Indians as an inferior race. They, like most of us, associated with people of their own social class, and they, like most of us, judged people on appearances. K.H. issued a stern warning to Sinnett about that tendency:

> Beware then, of an uncharitable spirit, for it will rise up like a hungry wolf in your path, and devour the better qualities of your nature that have been springing into life. Broaden instead of narrowing your sympathies; try to identify yourself with your fellows, rather than to contract your circle of affinity. (ML, letter 131, p. 435)

K.H. was trying yet again to impress Sinnett with the idea of a universal brotherhood of humanity, an idea that did not sit well with the white race at the time.

Although Sinnett may have had a tendency to dogmatism and to misconceptions about people, he was free of fixed ideas about religion and philosophy. Speaking of Sinnett and A. O. Hume, K.H. writes:

> Their beliefs are no barrier to us for they have *none*. They may have had influences around them, bad magnetic emanations the result of drink, Society and promiscuous physical associations (resulting even from shaking hands with impure men) but all this is physical and material impediments which with a little effort we could counteract and even clear away without much detriment to ourselves. Not so with the magnetism and invisible results proceeding from erroneous and sincere beliefs. . . . we would have to use more than ordinary exercise of power to drive them away. (ML, letter 30, p. 95)

When we become serious about trying to live a spiritual life, we are up against the mental and emotional inertia we have built up over years. We cannot expect to change our ways by repeating an affirmation in the morning and being transformed in the afternoon. A small amount of force may be overcome easily. Forty or fifty years of mental-emotional energy set moving in one direction cannot be reversed without applying a great deal more force than one short meditation or good intention. The body has its own consciousness and tends to act automatically. H.P.B. wrote of this in her ES *Instructions*:

> The flesh, the Body, the human being in his material part, is, on this plane, the most difficult thing to subject. The highest Adept, put into a new Body, has to struggle against and subdue it, and finds its subjugation difficult. But this is from the automatism of the Body; the original impulses have come from thought. What we call the desires of the Body have their origin in thought. Thought arises before desire. The thought acts on the Brain, the Lower Manas being the agent; the brain acts on the bodily organs, and then desire awakens. It is not the outer stimulus that arouses the bodily organs, but the Brain, impressed by a thought. Wrong thought must therefore be slain, ere desire can be extinguished. Desire is the outcome of separateness, aiming at the satisfaction of self in Matter. Now the flesh is a thing of habit; it will repeat mechanically a good impulse or a bad one, according to the impression made on it, and will continue to

repeat it. It is thus not the flesh which is the original tempter, although it may repeat automatically motions imparted to it, and so bring back temptations; in nine cases out of ten it is the Lower Manas which, by its images, leads the flesh into temptations. Then the Body automatically sets up repetitions. That is why it is not true that a man steeped in evil can, by sudden conversion, become as powerful for good as he was before for evil. His vehicle is too defiled, and he can at best but neutralize the evil, balancing up the bad Karmic causes he has set in motion, at any rate for that incarnation. You cannot take a herring/barrel and use it for attar of roses; the wood is too soaked through with the herring-drippings. When evil tendencies and impulses have been thoroughly impressed on the physical nature, they cannot at once be reversed. The molecules of the Body have been set in a Kâmic direction, and—though they have sufficient intelligence to discern between things on their own plane, *i.e.*, to avoid things harmful to themselves—they cannot understand a change of direction, the impulse to which comes from a higher plane. If they are too suddenly and too violently forced into a reverse action, disease, madness or death will result. (CW 12:692–693)

No doubt this is why K.H. advised Sinnett to "fill each day's measure with pure thoughts, wise words, kindly deeds" (LMW1:59).

Because of the consequences of what we might call mental

and emotional inertia, K.H. warned Sinnett about the enormous effort he would need to tread the path of occult science. He made it clear that treading the path was full of pitfalls and dangers and that one had to destroy what he called a "living wall," the wall of mental-emotional energy built up over many years. K.H. wrote:

> You were told, however, that the path to Occult Sciences has to be trodden laboriously and crossed at the danger of life; that every new step in it leading to the final goal is surrounded by pitfalls and cruel thorns; that the pilgrim who ventures upon it is made first to confront and *conquer* the thousand and one furies who keep watch over its adamantine gates and entrance—furies called Doubt, Skepticism, Scorn, Ridicule, Envy and finally Temptation—especially the latter; and that he who would see *beyond* had to first destroy this living wall; that he must be possessed of a heart and soul clad in steel, and of an iron, never failing determination and yet be meek and gentle, humble and have shut out from his heart every human passion, that leads to evil. Are / you all this? (ML, letter 126, pp. 422–423)

Of course Sinnett was not all that, nor are we, at least not yet. But if the Masters are right, we can become all that if we try and if we realize it will take selflessness, time, courage, and effort.

When K.H. says that we must shut out from our heart "every human passion," he most certainly does not mean that we should shut out every emotion. What the adept seems to be warning against is strong *personal* desire. He told Sinnett that too anxious expectation is not only tedious, but dangerous too. Each warmer and quicker throb of the heart wears so much of life away. The passions, the affections are not to be indulged in by him who seeks TO KNOW; for they "wear out the earthly body with their own secret power; and he, who would gain his aim—*must be cold*." He must not even desire too earnestly or too passionately the object he would reach: else, the very wish will prevent the possibility of its fulfillment, at best—retard and throw it back. (ML, letter 49, p. 137)

How nice it would be if we could ask K.H. to elaborate on what he meant by *cold*. Some have taken the statement a bit too literally and have tried to avoid even the simple pleasures of life. K.H. did not do that. He had a wonderful sense of humor and thoroughly enjoyed good music. Others have taken *cold* to mean that they should become uncaring. That would be the greatest of mistakes. Nevertheless, personal desire is insidious and can enter even the higher principles, where it becomes dangerous. Those who aspire to tread the path to adeptship sometimes forget that becoming an adept is almost a side effect of living to benefit humanity. Personal desire can contaminate spiritual longing. The only safe desire on the path is the desire to work with the adepts to help suffering humanity. As K.H. pointed out, if there is even a shadow of desire for self-benefit (specifically, becoming an adept), it is selfish in the eyes of the Masters.

In his statement to Sinnett, K.H. seems to have been using *affections* and *passions* as synonyms, and that may give us a clue to what he meant when he said that "the passions, the affections are not to be indulged in." *Passion* usually connotes unrestrained emotion, whereas *affection* may be a response to love. The latter may be "indulged in" even by an adept, as previously pointed out when K.H. said,

> I am still attracted towards *some* men more than toward others, and philanthropy . . . has never killed in me either individual preferences of friendship, love for my next of kin, or the ardent feeling of patriotism for the country in which I was last materially individualized. (ML, letter 15, p. 49)

Surely K.H. did not mean that we should kill our ardent feelings of patriotism or love for next of kin and friends.

According to the Buddha, human suffering originates in ignorance. That leads to identification with the *me*. That leads to selfishness, and selfishness leads to evil and suffering. K.H. elaborates on that by naming what he calls "three poisons" that prevent us from perceiving the spiritual portion of ourselves. Those poisons are anger, greed, and delusion. He adds to them what he calls the five obscurities, or obstructions: envy, passion, vacillation, sloth, and unbelief. He asks Sinnett to cherish lust and desire less if he would shorten the distance between them (ML, letter 47, p. 129).

Chapter 17

SELFISHNESS, PRIDE, AND EGOISM

In a letter to Mohini Chatterji, K.H. wrote, "Selfishness and the want of self-sacrifice are the greatest impediments on the path of adeptship" (LMW1:32). As does every religion, K.H. condemns selfishness and considers humility to be a virtue. In addition to selfishness, even the most subtle and unconscious kind, K.H. adds, "beware of Pride and Egoism, two of the worst snares for the feet of him who aspires to climb the high paths of Knowledge and Spirituality" (ML, letter 131, p. 436).

The Scottish poet Robert Burns wrote:

O wad some Power the giftie gie us
To see oursels as ithers see us
["O that God would give us the gift
to see ourselves as others see us"]

He wrote those lines after he had seen an incident in church. Near him sat a woman in her Sunday best finery. She noticed that several people were looking at her dress and she was flattered to think that they were admiring the dress. What she did not know was that there was a louse crawling up her dress, and the louse was the object of her neighbors' attention. Taking the incident for allegory, Burns used it as an illustration of the fact that we seldom if ever see ourselves as others see us. This is especially true for the cardinal sin of pride. When we are bragging about some personal achievement or about some honor bestowed upon us, it is usual to think that others are impressed. Frequently they are negatively impressed by our boastful pride rather than by our achievements. As *The Voice of the Silence* (verse 118) puts it: "Self-gratulation, O disciple, is like unto a lofty tower, up which a haughty fool has climbed. Thereon he sits in prideful solitude and unperceived by any but himself."

At the very beginning of his correspondence with Sinnett, K.H. listed some of the questions that Hume had submitted to him, and he commented on the motive behind Hume's alleged willingness to work with the Brothers. He wrote:

Now, what are your motives? . . . They are (1) The desire to receive positive and unimpeachable proofs that there really are forces in nature of which science knows nothing; (2) The hope to appropriate them some day—the sooner the better, for you do not like to wait—so as to enable yourself—(*a*) to demonstrate their existence to a few chosen western minds; (*b*) to contemplate future life as an objective reality built upon the rock of Knowledge—not of faith; and (*c*) to finally learn—most important this, among all your motives, perhaps, though the most occult and the best guarded—the whole truth about our Lodges and ourselves; to get, in short, the positive assurance that the "Brothers"—of whom everyone hears so much and sees so little—are real entities, not fictions of a disordered, hallucinated brain. . . . To our minds then, these motives, sincere and worthy of every serious consideration from the worldly standpoint, appear—*selfish*. . . . They are selfish because you must be aware that the chief object of the T.S. is not so much to gratify individual aspirations as to serve our fellow men; and the real value of this term "selfish," which may jar upon your ear, has a peculiar significance with us which it cannot have with you. . . . Perhaps you will better appreciate our meaning when told that in our view the highest aspirations for the welfare of humanity become tainted with selfishness if, in the mind of the philanthropist, there lurks the shadow of desire for self-benefit or a tendency to do injustice, even when these exist unconsciously to himself. Yet, you have ever discussed but to put down the idea of a universal Brotherhood, questioned its usefulness, and advised to remodel the T.S. on the principle of a college for the special study of occultism. This, my respected and esteemed friend and Brother—will never do! (ML, letter 2, pp. 7–8)

Selfishness to the adept is linked to motive, but if it is simply motive as we understand it, why should K.H. say the word has a "peculiar significance" to them? The solution to that question may be found in an example of how karma functions. Theoretically, there is a karmic response to every action, whether that action is physical, emotional, mental, or spiritual. There is no action or movement that does not produce a reaction. As an example, let us say that we toss a rock into the center of a large tub of water. Immediately we observe that ripples go out in all directions from the center to the edge of the tub. As soon as the ripples reach the edge of the tub, they begin to return to the center, to the very place at which the disturbance originated. Using that example as an imperfect, but still adequate, analogy, the center of the tub can represent the *me*. It is the personal ego, our center in kama-manas. If the *me* initiates the action, the consequences will ripple outward, ultimately affecting every molecule of water in the tub, but the place where the action began will suffer the greatest karmic consequences, the most powerful "bounce" in the water. The action is "selfish" because it originates from the personal self. If our action originates from the impersonal inner self, then the consequences do not return to the *me*. In the case of Sinnett and Hume, each had a personal reason for the action they proposed. True, they wanted to prove to the world that occult powers existed, but they wanted to be the ones to prove it and they wanted to prove it by first acquiring and then demonstrating those powers themselves.

As reprehensible as personal selfishness can be, there is what K.H. calls a more dangerous selfishness. He writes:

But there are persons, who, without ever showing any external sign of selfishness, are intensely selfish in their inner spiritual aspirations. These will follow the path / once chosen by them with their eyes closed to the interests of all but themselves, and see nothing outside the narrow pathway filled with their own personality. They are so intensely absorbed in the contemplation of their own supposed "righteousness" that nothing can ever appear right to them outside the focus of their own vision distorted by their self-complacent contemplation, and their judgment of the right and wrong. (ML, letter 134, pp. 441–442)

People who harbor inner selfishness will do whatever they think may be necessary to reach their goal. If they believe they can acquire spiritual knowledge and power by giving all they have to the poor, or by lying on a bed of nails, they will do it. They will do it for themselves alone. Their goal may be to become an adept, but like Sinnett and Hume, they want to reach that goal for themselves. Masking as altruism, such a goal often turns out to be selfish. Even the desire for nirvana can be a selfish desire. As K.H. puts it,

It is not the individual and determined purpose of attaining oneself Nirvana (the culmination of all knowledge and absolute wisdom) which is after all only an exalted and glorious *selfishness*—but the self-sacrificing pursuit of the best means to lead on the right path our neighbour, to cause as many of our fellow-creatures as we possibly can to benefit by it, which constitutes the true theosophist. (LMW1:3)

Chapter 18

DESIRE AND
ATTACHMENT

In Fragment I (verse 63) of *The Voice of the Silence*, we read:
"Kill out desire; but if thou killest it take heed lest from the
dead it should again arise." But if we had no desire to act,
we would become the living dead. Surely that is not what *The
Voice of the Silence* is suggesting. In directing us to "kill out desire," *The Voice of the Silence* is not asking us to kill out emotion.
If you read the Mahatma Letters, you will discover that Koot
Hoomi and Morya show strong feelings. They are not cold, emo-
tionless people.

Desire (kama) is the force that prods us into action. It is an
essential part of our nature, and as such it is neither good nor
bad. Acting generates karma, and from the karmic results of our
actions we can learn. Some have thought they should not act to
help others because they believe it is interfering with that person's karma. *The Voice of the Silence* (verse 135) tells us: "Inaction

in a deed of mercy becomes an action in a deadly sin." The problem arises not from action but from motive, so that we identify with desire and become attached to what we desire. The identity with desire produces craving for the objective and subjective objects of desire.

We may crave physical sensation, food, drink, companionship, prestige, power, or a soul mate. We may even crave fine art and music. It is the attachment to the objects of our craving that creates a problem, not the appreciation of them. To appreciate and enjoy fine art and music is not the same as craving fine art and music. In fact, K.H. claims that "music [is] the most divine and *spiritual* of arts" (ML, letter 85B, p. 264). It is the "I can't live without" feeling that reveals attachment, and it is attachment to the objects of our desires that causes us psychological pain. Although it is difficult to accept it, the indisputable fact is that everything changes, everything from our psychological states to the physical world. "This, too, shall pass away" has no exceptions, not even in the subjective realm of our own psyche. If we are attached to anything, even identified with it, psychological pain is inevitable when the object of our desire changes. How easy it is to see this, and yet how extraordinarily difficult it is to accept it.

From a scientific point of view as well as from a Theosophical point of view, everything in the objective world is moving, and moving equates to change. Nothing stays the same, even for a nanosecond. When we have what we want, we are happy. We don't want anything to change. But we can no more prevent our lives from changing than we can stop the earth from spinning on its axis. Our desire to keep things as they are, and the impossibility of doing so, produces psychological pain. Sages have told us that if we avoid becoming attached to the objects of our desire, it is possible to enjoy life to its fullest. Blavatsky once said that the Theosophist should have a deep appreciation of the sensate world, but a calm indifference to it. The indifference to the sensate world might be our complete acceptance of constant change. The appreciation of the sensate world might be our joy.

The following hypothetical example may help us to understand how our attachment to the objects of desire causes us pain. Let us say that we have planned out our day. Even if the tasks before us are unpleasant, we want our plan to go as we have set it up. We want to go through with it. We want to finish our work; we want to finish it on time; and we want to have a feeling of satisfaction with a job well done. Yet we are often frustrated, as the poet Robert Burns wrote in his poem "To a Mouse," whose house in an open field was destroyed by a plow: "The best-laid schemes o' mice an' men / Gang aft agley [often go awry]." When our plans are frustrated, we are likely to become upset. The upset comes because we are attached to the desire to have things go just as we planned them. Avoiding attachment to desire does not mean that we should not act. It would be foolish to say that we should do nothing or that we do not care about our plans. We do care. If our plans are blocked, however, can we accept that fact even if we are not happy about it? Can we ask: "What needs to be done now?" and get on with it without emotional upset? Can we say, "Few things matter much, and most things don't matter at all" and mean it? If we cannot, we are attached to and identified with our desire.

Whenever we feel angry, upset, fearful, anxious, or frustrated, we are reacting to blocked desire, kama. Anger and fear are responses to a threat of some kind. Kama is not only a desire to possess something; it is also a desire to reject something. We may desire to possess a lover, but we might just as well desire to be free of an enemy. Minor flare-ups of kama happen so often to most of us during the day that we are unaware of the tremendous influence those flare-ups have on our happiness and on that of those around us. Examples abound. Traffic jams, flight delays, jostling by crowds, loss of personal property, disruption of our daily routine, and much more provide opportunities for us to notice whether or not we are attached to our desires. If we feel that we must do something or become something or know something, we are likely attached to what we want. A Zen saying illustrates this: "There is really nothing you must be, and there is nothing you must do. There is really nothing you must have, and there is nothing you must know. There is really nothing you must become. However, it helps to understand that fire burns and that, when it rains, the earth gets wet."

Perhaps the most difficult attachment to avoid is the attachment to those we love. True love radiates out without personal hooks. Attachment is when we want to keep something or someone exactly as they are for our own emotional comfort. If we love a spouse or a friend without attachment, we can let them go when they move out of our lives or when they die. When we truly love someone, we want what is best for them; and sometimes what is best is that they die. Our grief, natural and nearly universal among us, is evidence that in addition to our love, we have become attached to having their physical presence with us.

Does nonattachment to desire mean that we should not plan? Nothing could be further from the truth. Planning for one's future is common sense. Death, the greatest change of all, is inevitable. It would be foolish to ignore that fact, and even more foolish not to prepare for it. Knowing something of inevitable cycles, we can plan ahead. Our plans may or may not work out as we hope, but that should not prevent us from being as sensible as possible.

Once we realize that psychological pain is caused by craving and attachment, we may want to search for a way to end craving. If we are also motivated by what we might call a "holy" desire to live the Golden Stairs, we may search for instructions on how to live that life. We may be tempted to think that if we learn the rules and follow the instructions, we will graduate as college students graduate after they pass all their required courses. Unfortunately, there are no step-by-step instructions for treading the spiritual path. The path is your life. We must change ourselves, and no one else can do that for us.

It may help us to understand that if we think over our life from childhood to the present day. What was once so important to us at age seven is totally unimportant now at age fifty-seven. We have changed. As *The Voice of the Silence* (verse 58) puts it: "Thou canst not travel on the Path before thou hast become that Path itself." And as the Spanish poet Antonio Machado puts it:

"*Caminante, no hay camino. / Se hace camino al andar.*" (Traveler, there is no road. One makes the road by traveling.)

The goal is the same for all, but the route to it is your life, and each individual life is unique. The next step for one person is not the next step for another. Once again *The Voice of the Silence* (verse 197) puts it well: "The Path is one for all, the means to reach the goal must vary with the Pilgrims." Although the means to reach the goal will vary with each individual pilgrim, there are guidelines that can point the way. Among them is what has been called "the three limbs" of the Theosophical life: study, meditation, and service.

Chapter 19

STUDY, MEDITATION,
AND SERVICE

The Masters did not call study, meditation, and service the three limbs of the Theosophical life, but they and Blavatsky emphasized the need for all three. Blavatsky summed up the need for study and meditation: "By perfection in study and meditation the Supreme Spirit becomes manifest; study is one eye to behold it, and meditation is the other" (*Gems from the East: A Birthday Book of Precepts and Axioms*, compiled by H.P.B., in CW 12:439). Both H.P.B. and the Masters also emphasized that an altruistic life, a life of service, defines the true Theosophist. Study, meditation, and service are inseparably linked together, but in order to understand them from a Theosophical perspective, we must look at each in turn.

STUDY

We can study anything under the sun, but the subject of Theosophical study is summed up in the second object of the Society (as it is phrased in the *Quest* journal of the Theosophical Society in America): to encourage the comparative study of religion, philosophy, and science. To begin our study, it would be helpful to study the primary literature of the Theosophical movement because Blavatsky taught that Theosophy is not a religion, but religion itself. In a statement published in the international journal of the Theosophical Society (on the back of the contents page), Theosophy is defined in part as "the body of truths which forms the basis of all religions, and which cannot be claimed as the exclusive possession of any. . . . It illuminates the scriptures and doctrines of religion by unveiling their hidden meanings, and thus justifying them at the bar of intelligence, as they are ever justified in the eyes of intuition." For those unfamiliar with Theosophy, Blavatsky's *Key to Theosophy* would be a good starting place. Or, if one prefers a contemporary statement of Theosophical principles, Edward Abdill's *The Secret Gateway*, John Algeo's *Theosophy: An Introductory Study Course*, and other introductory books and courses on Theosophy are available.

When we move on to a comparative study of religion, we are apt to discover among the various religions similar myths and a code of ethics that emphasizes a way of life filled with compassion. Naturally, we will find many differences as well, and we must not gloss over those differences or erroneously conclude that all religions are the same. Yet in the mystical and esoteric literature of the great religious traditions, the similarities are greater than the differences. Finally, while there is no need to become scientists or philosophers, we might keep informed about the latest scientific discoveries that may provide evidence supporting Theosophical theory. Since the motto of the Theosophical Society is "There is no religion higher than truth," we must also note any evidence that contradicts Theosophical theories.

The method of studying spiritual literature is not the same as the method we use to study instruction manuals. The latter are specific and literal. If we try to read instruction manuals as we would read poetry, we will surely be confused. We must follow their directions as written. But spiritual literature needs a different approach. Reading and remembering the words in a spiritual book is not the same as understanding what has been written. Spiritual literature is seldom to be taken literally. It frequently uses poetry and metaphor to express meaning that the words themselves cannot communicate. This is not to say that we should never take the words literally. We must learn to distinguish what is meant literally and what is meant allegorically or metaphorically. If everyone approached spiritual literature in that way, much of the strife among people of different religions might be eliminated because religious conflict occurs mostly among fundamentalists who believe that their scriptures are literally true.

Annie Besant once said that we should read a little and think a lot. Being well read is not a bad thing in itself. What is bad is intellectual gluttony. If we gulp down as much food as we can in a short time, we don't digest the food properly. If we try to read as many books as we can in the shortest possible time, we don't "digest" the knowledge properly. In both cases, we gain little and harm our physical or mental health in the process. In studying spiritual literature, we should do as Annie Besant suggests: read a little and think a lot. If we do not understand an intriguing passage in a book such as *The Voice of the Silence*, we can meditate on it. Rather than approaching the passage intellectually, as we must do with mundane problems, we can simply focus on the thought and let it sit in our mind quietly as we ponder, seeking to understand it. The thought may remain in the back of our mind for hours, days, or even longer. Then one day, when our mind is quiet, the light of understanding may flash on our minds from that universal state we call buddhi. If instead we try to analyze the passage, we will be peeling the proverbial onion. Rather than understanding the meaning, we will be left with tears of frustration and only bits and pieces of what was once an onion. Study in the Theosophical sense is a type of meditation. It opens the mind to spiritual insight.

MEDITATION

Many practices have been called "meditation." Some are useful, some are useless, and some are harmful. To begin to understand what true meditation is, we might consider what meditation is not.

Because we are one-pointed in consciousness, we cannot *consciously* focus on two things at the same time. We can focus on a book we are reading and at the same time be aware of what surrounds the book, but we cannot focus on the foreground and the background at the same time. This is true in meditation also. Although the ability to concentrate is essential in meditation, concentration is not meditation.

Some people like to play recorded music while they meditate. Music has been used successfully in spiritual practices and healing for ages. Soothing, harmonious music can calm the mind and the emotions. Yet because we are one-pointed in consciousness, we cannot focus on the music and meditate at the same time. We can center our consciousness on one or the other, but not on both simultaneously. We might best use music as a preparation for meditation and then meditate in silence.

Meditation is not self-hypnosis. It is not a way of putting ourselves in a trancelike state. Although using creative imagination may be a useful tool of meditation, meditation is not imagining ourselves in another place. It is not otherworldly. We do not go anywhere in meditation. In fact, we become more centered within ourselves and our whole nature becomes more integrated, our mind more alert. Meditation profoundly affects the emotions, but meditation is not an emotion-centered activity. Neither is it a method to achieve something we want, even if that something is inner peace. Whatever begins with the personal ego, ends there. Once when Jiddu Krishnamurti was asked, "Is there a road from here to there?" he answered, "Sir, there is a road, but it is not from here to there. It is from there to here." At first that may be difficult to comprehend, but as our meditations become more profound, the truth of that statement may become clear. Meditation is not thought and most especially it is not words. The library at the Theosophical Society in America has a free bookmark that reads, "Meditation is not what you think." If we simply think thoughts such as "I am sending peace to the world," it will do no good unless we focus on and feel peace within ourselves and then consciously radiate it to the world. The words themselves are necessary only to communicate to others a suggested action in meditation. Once the action is understood, the words must be dropped. H.P.B. defined meditation as the inexpressible longing of the inner self for the infinite. Putting it another way, she said, "Meditation is silent and unuttered prayer, or, as Plato expressed it, 'the ardent turning of the soul toward the divine; not to ask any particular good (as in the common meaning of prayer), but for good itself—for the universal Supreme Good' of which we are a part on earth, and out of the essence of which we have all emerged" (Key to Theosophy, p. 10). If union with the divine is your goal in meditation, you can't go wrong. It is the lodestar that will lead you in the right direction, always away from self and toward the Eternal.

Krishnamurti accurately described meditation as follows: "Meditation is a process of emptying the mind of all the activity of the self, of all the activity of the 'me.' If you do not understand the activity of the self, then your meditation only leads to illusion, your meditation then only leads to self-deception, your meditation then will only lead to further distortion. So to understand what meditation is, you must understand the activity of the self" (from *The Light in Oneself*, at www.jkrishnamurti .org/krishnamurti-teachings/view-daily-quote/20091126.php?t =Meditation).

There are two essential aspects of meditation. First, we must learn to quiet the mind. When first attempting to meditate, many people say that they cannot do it because their minds fill with thought. Recognizing that fact is not failure; it is a step forward. We try to clear our mind and the vacuum sucks in thoughts from our subconscious. Until that moment, we did not realize how many thoughts wait for an opening into the conscious mind. Now the goal must be to allow those thoughts to die.

To rid the mind of thought is not easy, but it is not as difficult as one might suppose. Occasionally we all get a melody into our heads that to our annoyance keeps repeating itself. Let us say it is a singing commercial that we have heard on television. We do not even like the tune, but we can't seem to stop hearing it. Now think back to a day when that happened to you. How did that melody die? Almost certainly you will realize that when your attention was drawn away from it, the melody began to fade away. Unconsciously you were giving the melody energy by focusing your attention on it. The only life it had was your conscious attention. Once you got a phone call or were interrupted in some other way, your attention was taken off the melody and it began to die. It is the same with thoughts that enter our mind during meditation.

Thoughts that enter our mind during meditation attract our attention and we begin to follow those thoughts, creating a chain of thought that takes us far from our intended goal. When we realize that we have been drawn away by thought, there is a tendency to think that we cannot meditate. If we remember how an annoying melody in our mind died, we will realize that the thoughts in our mind will die in the same way: by taking our conscious attention away from them and focusing on the object of our meditation. Thoughts will die a natural death if we do that. They will only be intensified if we focus on and follow them.

It is important to remember that, during the process of clearing our mind of thought, we stay focused on the goal of discovering and uniting with the Eternal. That will prevent creating a vacuum in the mind. Nature abhors a vacuum, and that principle is evident even in our mind. The following passage in the New Testament, Matthew 12:43–45, may be warning us not to leave our mind blank because if we do, we will soon find our mind filled with many unwanted thoughts:

> When the unclean spirit is gone out of a man, he walketh through dry places, seeking rest, but findeth none. / Then he saith, "I will return into my house from whence I came out." And when he is come, he findeth it empty, swept, and garnished. / Then goeth he, and taketh with himself seven other spirits more wicked than himself, and they enter in and dwell there: And the last state of that man is worse than the first.

In 1876, the mental healer Warren Felt Evans coined the phrase, "thoughts are things." It was later popularized by journalist Prentice Mulford. Master Koot Hoomi agreed with that phrase and added to it. He wrote, "thoughts are things—have tenacity, coherence and life . . . they are real entities" (ML, letter 18, p. 66). When thoughts leave us, they become ensouled by elementals. That is, they become living entities, or what the scripture called "spirits." With little intelligence, these living thoughts reside in the lower nature and may tend more toward ill than good. Hence it is possible to interpret "unclean spirit" as a carnal thought. If we create a vacuum in our mind, we open ourselves to anything that might be sucked into that vacuum. Keeping the positive intent of union with the Eternal will keep our mind from being invaded by unwanted guests.

The second aspect of meditation is to discover within ourselves a place of absolute stillness. That stillness is not the stillness of the graveyard. Rather it is a living stillness. It is the stillness and peace of Eternity. It has been beautifully described by a Zen master as "a fleeting forever" because in a timeless flash there is no *me*, there is no time, there is only the Eternal. The Christian mystic Meister Eckhart commented that since all arose from nothing, nothing is our true home. Eternity is no thing; at the same time, the potential for everything is within it. T. S. Eliot has also described the experience as "to arrive where we started / And know the place for the first time" ("Little Gidding," V). For at least a moment, the inner self has awakened and the personality is humbled before it.

H.P.B. described the experience:

In his hours of silent meditation the student will find that there is one space of silence within him where he can find refuge from thoughts and desires, from the turmoil of the

senses and the delusions of the mind. By sinking his consciousness deep into his heart he can / reach this place—at
first only when he is alone in silence and darkness. But when
the need for the silence has grown great enough, he will turn
to seek it even in the midst of the struggle with self, and he
will find it. Only he must not let go of his outer self, or his
body; he must learn to retire into this citadel when the battle
grows fierce, but to do so without losing sight of the battle;
without allowing himself to fancy that by so doing he has
won the victory. That victory is won only when all is silence
without as within the inner citadel. (CW 8:127–128)

When we have touched the "inner citadel," awakened even for
a moment the inner self, we never forget it. Our problems do not
go away, but we are able to handle them more effectively. We may
and likely will continue to go through difficult times, times of
grief, sorrow, and pain, but we will never forget that within we
are rooted in eternal peace and we will pass through difficulties
more easily than we would have before we entered the citadel.

Meditating in this way has a profound effect on us. It integrates the whole person. Blavatsky tells us:

If . . . man proceeding on his life-journey looked . . . *within
himself* and centered his point of observation on the *inner*
man, he would soon escape from the coils of the great serpent
of illusion. From the cradle to the grave, his life would then
become supportable and worth living, even in its worst phases.
(CW 8:116)

For more on the practice of meditation, see below, Appendix 2: Meditation.

SERVICE

In *The Voice of the Silence* (verse 144), we are told: "To live to benefit mankind is the first step." Yet only a small number of individuals seem to do much for humanity. Prominent among those are a few scientists, politicians, and philanthropists. We might reasonably ask, "How can I, an average person, live to benefit humanity?"

Service in the Theosophical sense means selfless action for the greater good. It does not mean that we have to change the world single-handedly. Service is an attitude of mind and action. We can all be conscious of how our thoughts, feelings, and actions affect others. When a need arises, we must first determine whether we can help. Frequently, there is nothing we can do. For example, if we live in a large city, we may see a fair number of homeless people. It tears at our hearts to see the suffering, but we cannot take in every homeless person. Perhaps we can volunteer at a soup kitchen or contribute to a charitable organization that provides food and shelter. Perhaps we can do neither, and if so, we must accept that. Annie Besant once said that if we cannot do a particular work, that work is not our work. We can only do what we are capable of doing and must not be sentimental about work we cannot do.

Service is much more an attitude of mind than any particular action. A kind word to a supermarket clerk is service. Stopping to help someone who has fallen on the street is service. Cheering up a bereaved friend is service. There are countless opportunities every day to serve.

Study, meditation, and service are interconnected. The first two result in the last. Service becomes part of our nature. We cannot stand by if we see a need we know we can fill. To do nothing would violate our nature. The combination of study and meditation has changed us. It has awakened our spiritual nature. It has awakened compassion in us, and compassion is the motivating power behind service.

We can be fairly certain that compassionate service arises from meditation and service, but we cannot say that it arises *only* from meditation and service. In fact, there is some evidence that compassion is so rooted in nature that it may even be present in some animals. Both domestic and wild animals show some startling examples of what may be compassionate behavior, but because animals cannot describe their feelings to us, it is possible that their behavior is a response to something else in their nature. Whether or not compassion exists generally in nature, it most certainly exists in human nature. Furthermore, compassionate action has a domino effect. Our acting compassionately seems to stimulate others into acting compassionately.

Chapter 20

LAY CHELAS
AND CHELAS

The term *chela* translates roughly as "student." That term, however, has a specific meaning to the Masters. It refers to individuals whose highly developed spiritual qualities have attracted the attention of a Master who has consequently taken such an individual under his wing as a student.

The Gospel of St. Matthew (22:14) states: "For many are called, but few are chosen." For chelas, we might paraphrase that as "For many *aspire* to become chelas, but few are chosen." Those who are chosen have already put the greater good before their own. K.H. wrote to a member: "The true Theosophist is a philanthropist—'Not for himself but for the world he lives'" (LMW1:76). In pointing out how to come into the sphere of the Master's influence, K.H. wrote that: "the aim of the philanthropist should be the spiritual enlightenment of his fellow-men, and whoever works unselfishly to that goal necessarily puts himself in magnetic communication with our chelas and *our-*

selves" (LMW1:75). K.H. added: "The moral and spiritual sufferings of the world are more important and need help and cure more than science needs aid from us in any field of discovery" (LMW1:77). As *The Voice of the Silence* (verse 144) puts it, "To live to benefit mankind is the first step." Obviously, the first step is far too difficult for most people to climb.

Ever since H.P.B. introduced the Brothers to the Western world, there have been individuals who desire to meet a Master and become students. Being conditioned by Western education, many of these aspirants seem to think that a Master will respond to their desire to be taught in the same way that a university would accept them as students. Most aspirants do not know what is required of them to become chelas, or even candidates, of an adept.

According to H.P.B.:

A Lay Chela is but a man of the world who affirms his desire to become wise in spiritual things. Virtually, every member of the Theosophical Society who subscribes to the second of our three "Declared Objects" is such; for though not of the number of true Chelas, he has yet the possibility of becoming one, for he has stepped across the boundary line which separated him from the Mahatmas, and has brought himself, as it were, under their notice. In joining the Society and binding himself to help along its work, he has pledged himself to act in some degree in concert with those Mahatmas, at whose behest the Society was organized, and under whose conditional protection it remains. The joining is then, the introduction; all the rest depends entirely upon the member himself, and he need never expect the most distant approach to . . . one of our Mahatmas . . . that has not been fully earned by personal merit . . . LAY CHELASHIP CONFERS NO PRIVILEGE UPON ANYONE EXCEPT THAT OF WORKING FOR MERIT UNDER THE OBSERVATION OF A MASTER. And whether that Master be or be not seen by the Chela makes no difference whatever as to the result: his good thought, words and deeds will bear their fruits, his evil ones, theirs. To boast of Lay Chelaship or make a parade of it, is the surest way to reduce the relationship with the Guru to a mere empty name, for it would be *prima facie* evidence of vanity and unfitness for further progress. And for years we have been teaching everywhere the maxim "First deserve, then desire" intimacy with the Mahatmas. (CW 4:610–611)

H.P.B. has described the qualifications to become a "lay chela." The qualifications to become a true chela are much more stringent, and there is a good reason for that. There is a close magnetic link between a Master and a full chela. Therefore the Master will be affected by whatever that chela thinks, feels, or does. Obviously, the adepts would not want to link anyone to themselves who is not completely pure morally and who is strong enough to withstand the blows and temptations of life in the everyday world. Therefore, before accepting a lay chela as a full chela, the aspirant is put on probation.

The probationary period begins almost as soon as one aspires to become a chela. K.H. tells us "that he who approaches our precincts even in thought, is drawn into the vortex of probation" (ML, letter 131, p. 435). Because the Masters are not omniscient, they cannot know whether or not the aspirant will be successful until he or she has been thoroughly tested. The tests will not be artificially created by the adept. Life will provide its own trials and all the adept need do is to observe how the aspirant handles those trials. K.H. explains the first step of the probationary period:

> The aspirant is now assailed entirely on the psychological side of his nature. His course of testing—in Europe and India—is that of Raj-yog and its result is—as frequently explained—to develop every germ good and bad in him in his temperament. The rule is inflexible, and not one escapes whether he but writes to us a letter, or in the privacy of his own heart's thought formulates a strong desire for occult communication and knowledge. As the shower cannot fructify the rock, so the occult teaching has no effect upon the unreceptive mind; and as the water develops the heat of caustic lime so does the teaching bring into fierce action every unsuspected potentiality latent in him. (ML, letter 136, pp. 451–452)

The psychological assault takes the form of inner struggles against fear, depression, anxiety, and a host of problems that come as threats to the personal ego. In our effort to live the life the Masters tell us is necessary, we may become discouraged to the point of giving up. To pass the tests we must have an iron and never-failing will.

The period of probation may last for some years, and it draws out the latent best and worst in the candidate, of whom the old saying may apply that "fools rush in where angels fear to tread" (from Alexander Pope's "An Essay on Criticism"). Once candidates are informed of the following requirements, few would press on:

1. Perfect physical health. 2. Absolute mental and physical purity. 3. Unselfishness of purpose, universal charity, pity for all animate beings. 4. Truthfulness and unswerving faith in the law of karma, independent of any power in nature that could interfere: a law whose course is not to be obstructed by any agency, not to be caused to deviate by prayer or propitiatory exoteric ceremonies. 5. A courage undaunted in every emergency, even by peril to life. 6. An intuitional perception of one's being the vehicle of the manifested Avalokiteshvara or Divine Atman (Spirit). 7. Calm indifference for, but a just appreciation of, everything that constitutes the objective and transitory world in its relationship with the invisible regions. . . . With the sole exception of the first, which in rare and exceptional cases might have been modified, each one of these points has been invariably insisted upon, and all must have been more or less developed in the inner nature by the Chela's UNHELPED EXERTIONS, before he could be actually put to the test. (CW 4:608)

What may surprise many is the fact that the adepts prefer to have a chela strongly disagree with them rather than simply accept without question everything the adept says. K.H. puts this in a way that will shock many:

> The chela is at perfect liberty, *and often quite justified from the standpoint of appearances*—to suspect his Guru of being "a fraud" as the elegant word stands. More than that: the greater, the sincerer his indignation—whether expressed in words or boiling in his heart—the more fit he is, the better qualified to become an *adept*. He is free to [use], and will not be held to account for using the most abusive words and expressions regarding his guru's actions and orders, provided he comes out victorious from the fiery ordeal; provided he resists all and every temptation; rejects every allurement, and proves that nothing, not even the promise of that which he holds dearer than life, of that most precious boon, his future adeptship—is able to make him deviate from the path of truth and honesty, or force him to become a *deceiver*. (ML, letter 74, p. 222)

This statement becomes more understandable when we remember that the chela knows that the Master is human and therefore is subject to error. In the end, chelas must stand on their own feet, not relying on a Master or a God. It is self-sufficiency that the Masters want, and they do whatever they can to strengthen that in their chelas. Candidates may conquer all their trials so long as they are not overconfident of success.

Commenting on the requirements for chelaship, *The Voice of the Silence* (verse 137) tells us: "Have patience, Candidate, as one who fears no failure, courts no success. Fix thy Soul's gaze upon the star whose ray thou art, the flaming star that shines within the lightless depths of ever-being, the boundless fields of the Unknown."

K.H. warns of the dangers of possible failure when he writes:

Chelaship *unveils* the *inner* man and draws forth the dormant vices as well as the dormant virtue. Latent vice begets active sins and is often followed by insanity. Out of 5 lay chelas chosen by the Society and accepted under protest by *us*, 3 have become criminals and 2 are insane. . . . Be pure, virtuous, and lead a holy life and you will be protected. But remember, he who is not as pure as a young child better leave chelaship alone. . . . The process of self-purification is not the work of a moment, nor of a few months, but of years, nay, extending over a series of lives. The later a man begins living the higher life the longer must be his period of probation. For he has to undo the effects of a long number of years spent in objects diametrically opposed to the real goal. (LMW1:31)

Another unexpected consequence of becoming a chela is that karma is speeded up. K.H. tells Sinnett:

The mass of human sin and frailty is distributed throughout the life of man who is content to remain an average mortal. It is gathered in and centered, so to say, within one period of the life of a chela—the period of probation. That which is generally accumulating to find its legitimate issue only in the next rebirth of an ordinary man, is quickened and fanned into existence in the chela—especially in the presumptuous and selfish candidate who rushes in without having calculated his forces. (ML, letter 134, p. 441)

Chelas under probation often expect guidance from their Master, but K.H. states otherwise: "we never *guide* our chelas (the most advanced even); nor do we forewarn them, leaving the effects produced by causes of their own creation to teach them better experience" (ML, letter 95, p. 333). K.H. also wrote:

The fact is, that to the last and supreme initiation every chela—(and even some adepts)—is left to his own device and counsel. We have to fight our own battles, and the familiar adage—"the adept *becomes*, he is not *made*" is true to the letter. Since every one of us is the *creator* and producer of the *causes* that lead to such or some other *results*, we have to reap but what we have sown. *Our chelas are helped but when they are innocent of the causes that lead them into trouble;* when such causes are generated by foreign, outside influences. Life and the struggle for adeptship would be too easy, had we all scavengers behind us to sweep away the *effects* we have generated through our own rashness and presumption. Before they are allowed to go into the world they—the chelas—are every one of them endowed with more or less clairvoyant powers; and, with the exception of that faculty that, unless paralyzed and

watched would lead them perchance to divulge certain secrets that must not be revealed—they are left in the full exercise of their powers—whatever these may be. . . . Thus, step
by step, and after a series of punishments, is the chela taught
by bitter experience to suppress and guide his impulses;
he loses his rashness, his self-sufficiency and never falls into
the same errors. . . . I must remind you of that which you
so heartily hate; namely, that no one comes in contact with
us, no one shows a desire to know more of us, but has to
submit to being tested and put by us on probation. (ML, letter 92, p. 294)

When K.H. says that the chela must go through a series
of punishments, he does not mean that anyone, including the
Master, is punishing the chela. It is the karma of our actions that
result in what K.H. called "punishments." It is the consequences
of our own misguided actions that bring pain. The so-called
punishments are the lawful reactions to our actions. Those who
hold a simplistic view of karma would probably be surprised
to read that anyone can be "innocent of the causes that lead them
into trouble." The popular view of karma is that everything that
happens to us comes from our own actions. Obviously, the Master disagrees with that. The adepts say that they never interfere
with karma, so if we have set a cause in motion that results in
an unpleasant reaction for us, the Master will not interfere, but
everything that happens to us is *not* our fault. There is no action
of any kind that is not under the fundamental law of karma, but
karma is not tit-for-tat. If we encounter difficulties that are not

of our own making, the balance will be set straight at some future time or in some future incarnation. In the case of full chelas, the Master is likely to protect his students from unmerited harm, but by doing so he is not violating karmic law, because that would be impossible. He is merely taking action that will protect his chelas from attack or danger that the chelas did not bring upon themselves.

Although the adepts will not protect us from ourselves, they do influence people, especially their chelas. K.H. wrote:

Every human being contains within himself vast potentialities, and it is the duty of the adepts to surround the would-be chela with circumstances which shall enable him to take the "right-hand path,"—if he have the ability in him. We are no more at liberty to withhold the chance from a postulant than we are to guide and direct him into the proper course. At best, we can only show him—after his probation period was successfully terminated—that if he does this he will go right; if the other, wrong. But until he has passed that period, we leave him to fight out his battles as best he may; . . . we allow our candidates *to be tempted* in a thousand various ways, so as to draw out the whole of their inner nature and allow it the chance of remaining conqueror either one way or the other. . . . The victor's crown is only for him who proves himself worthy to wear it; for him who attacks *Mara* single handed and conquers the demon of lust and earthly passions; and not *we* but he himself puts it on his brow. It was not a meaningless phrase of the Tathagata [the Buddha] that "he who masters *Self* is greater than he who conquers thousands in battle": there is no such other difficult struggle. If it were not so, adeptship would be but a cheap acquirement. (ML, letter 92, p. 299)

After giving stern warnings about the dangers associated with chelaship and after outlining the qualities required in the would-be chela, K.H. adds a word of encouragement: "We have one word for all aspirants: TRY" (ML, letter 54, p. 148).

Chapter 21

WORKING AS
COLLEAGUES WITH
THE MASTERS

Many wonder if the Masters are alive today, and if so, whether they are still communicating with individuals. Since the letter that K.H. wrote to Annie Besant in 1900, we have no proof that anyone is still receiving letters from the Masters. There is some evidence, however, that at least one person, Dora van Gelder Kunz, was in direct contact with them in the latter part of the twentieth century.

Dora was born into a Theosophical family in Java, Dutch East Indies, on April 28, 1904. She died on August 25, 1999. Dora was born with clairvoyant ability to a mother who was also clairvoyant. Until Dora was older, she thought that everyone saw what she saw because she and her mother both saw the same things. When she was only eleven years old, C. W. Leadbeater asked her parents if she could accompany him to Australia, where he wanted to train sensitive young people to develop further their clairvoyant ability in a Theosophical setting. Dora's parents told her to go to their meditation room, think about the proposal, and decide whether or not to go. Dora was a shy girl who did not speak English. Her parents never thought she would decide to go to Australia, but to their great surprise she did.

When she was in her early twenties, Dora met Fritz Kunz. Fritz was an American who had been traveling with Leadbeater. Soon she traveled with Fritz to the United States, where they were married. Both she and Fritz were dedicated members of the Theosophical Society. The two could not have been more different in their personalities. Fritz was dedicated to justifying Theosophical philosophy with modern science, and Dora was dedicated to helping people in physical and psychological need. In the early 1970s, she and Dr. Dolores Krieger developed Therapeutic Touch, an energy therapy. It was Dora who could see the energy flowing through the body, and it was Dolores who gave the practice its name and introduced it into nursing schools and hospitals.

Dora frequently lectured for the Theosophical Society on healing, meditation, and the Masters. She was thoroughly dedicated to the Masters and to the Society. Her husband once said of her, "If there is one word that would describe my wife, it is duty." Those of us who knew her agree. Dora, like the Masters, put duty above all else. In a letter to Sinnett, K.H. put it plainly when he spoke of duty to his Master:

But my first duty is to *my* Master. And duty, let me tell you, is for us stronger than any friendship or even love; as without this abiding principle which is the indestructible cement that has held together for so many millenniums, the scattered custodians of nature's grand secrets—our Brotherhood, nay, our doctrine itself—would have crumbled long ago into unrecognisable atoms. (ML, letter 126, p. 422)

The Masters say that their chelas must be endowed with clairvoyant ability, and Dora was one of the most gifted clairvoyants of modern times. What evidence we have for Dora's relationship with the Masters comes from her nature and from a few incidents in her life. Whenever Dora spoke for the Society, she would say: "I am not speaking from books. I am speaking from my own experience." Although she had an enormous vocabulary, was well read, was thoroughly familiar with Theosophical literature, and knew American history better than most Americans, her strength was not in words. Often she would mix metaphors and seldom finish a sentence. When dealing with her work, however, she was exceedingly careful and would never come to any conclusion until she had thoroughly investigated the matter under study. In listening to Dora, one somehow understood what she meant in spite of her misuse of words.

Given the fact that Dora would never talk about anything beyond her experience, her 1955 Philadelphia lecture on the Masters is especially striking. Appendix 1 is a slightly edited transcript of that lecture. In that talk, Dora described how one feels in the presence of K.H. and Morya. She even described their facial expressions. Such detailed descriptions are not in any Theosophical literature, and Dora would never have described the Masters if she had not seen them.

It is possible that Dora was a chela. K.H. told Sinnett that a full chela and even their direct agent, H.P.B., had to have one of their principles removed and kept with the Masters. We have no explanation for just what that means, but the results, according to K.H.'s explanation for Blavatsky's difficult personality, was that it made her a psychological cripple unable fully to control her personality. That was exactly the case with Dora Kunz. When she spoke of the Masters, it was as though the Masters were present with her. She was a spiritual giant with a difficult personality. She and H.P.B. were both like the little girl with the curl. When they were good they were very, very good. But when they were bad they were horrid.

It was alleged by some that Rukmini Devi Arundale was a chela. She was also a spiritual giant and a difficult personality. When Rukmini died, Dora was president of the Theosophical Society in America, living at the T.S. headquarters in Wheaton, Illinois. When Dora was informed that Rukmini died, she gasped and said, "I'm the last one." The last one what? One can think of no other explanation except that both were students of one of the Masters. While living at Olcott, the Theosophical Society headquarters, a staff member once walked by Dora's room in the wee hours of the morning and heard Dora, alone in her room, saying, "I *am* trying. I *am* trying." The word *try* was used many times by the Masters, and it was conceivable that one of them was with her in some form to teach and encourage her that night.

Although we have no evidence that anyone is in direct contact with the Masters today, that does not mean the Masters are not in contact with a chosen few. Almost certainly those few, like Dora Kunz, would not make any claim of personal contact. The Masters have told us that anyone who aspires to work with them for humanity will come into rapport with them, and that is just as valid today as it was in the nineteenth century. We may say, "What can I possibly do to help a mahatma?" The question is reasonable, but when we realize that we can come into rapport with the Master's work, we will realize that we can be helpful, and that it does not matter at all whether or not the Master is still incarnate in the same body he used in the nineteenth century. Therefore, we may safely assume that what K.H. wrote to Sinnett about coming into rapport with a Master is true for us today. K.H. reassured Sinnett and us when he wrote:

Your strivings, perplexities and forebodings are equally noticed, good and faithful friend. In the imperishable RE-CORD of the Masters *you have written them all.* There are registered your every deed and thought; for, though not a chela, as you say to my Brother Morya, nor even a "protégé"— as you understand the term—still, you have stepped within the circle of our work, you have crossed the mystic line which separates your world from ours. . . . In thought and deed, by day, in soul-struggles by nights, you have been writing the story of your desires and your spiritual development. This, every one does who approaches us with any earnestness of desire to become our co-worker; he himself "precipitates" the written entries by the identical process used by us when we write inside your closed letters and uncut pages of books and pamphlets in transit. . . . During the past few months, especially, when your weary brain was plunged in the torpor of sleep, your eager soul has often been searching after me, and the current of your thought been beating against my protecting barriers. . . . If you hear seldom from me, never feel disappointed, my Brother, but say—"It is *my* fault." Nature has linked all parts of her Empire together by subtle threads of magnetic sympathy, and, there is a mutual correlation even between a star and a man; thought runs swifter than the electric fluid, and your thought *will find me* if projected by a pure impulse, as mine will find, has found, and often impressed your mind. We may move in cycles of activity divided—not entirely separated from each other. Like the light in the sombre valley seen by the mountaineer from his peaks, every bright thought in your mind, my Brother, will sparkle and attract the attention of your distant friend and correspondent. . . . and it is our law to approach every such an one if even there be but the feeblest glimmer of the true "Tathagata" light [the light of the Buddha] within him—then how far easier for you to attract us. Understand this and the admission into the Society of persons often distasteful to you will no longer amaze you. "They that be whole need not the physician, but they that be sick"—is an axiom, whoever may have spoken it. (ML, letter 47, pp. 131–132)

Living the altruistic life will bring us into rapport with the adepts. K.H. made this crystal clear when he wrote:

It is he alone who has the love of humanity at heart, who is capable of grasping thoroughly the idea of a regenerating practical Brotherhood who is entitled to the possession of our secrets. He alone, such a man—will never misuse his powers, as there will be no fear that he should turn them to selfish ends. A man who places / not the good of mankind above his own good is not worthy of becoming our *chela*—he is not worthy of becoming higher in knowledge than his neighbour. If he craves for phenomena let him be satisfied with the pranks of spiritualism. (ML, letter 33, pp. 100–101)

Often aspirants think that the Masters are free to select anyone they choose as a potential chela. In one sense that is true, but the selection does not depend on the Master's *personal* will. Explaining that to C. W. Leadbeater, K.H. wrote:

To accept any man as a chela does not depend on my personal will. It can only be the result of one's personal merit and exertions in that direction. *Force* any one of the "Masters" you may happen to choose; do good works in his name and for the love of mankind; be pure and resolute in the path of righteousness (as laid out in *our* rules); be honest and unselfish; forget your Self but to remember the good of other people—and you will have *forced* that "Master" to accept you. (LMW1:28)

There is another way we can come into rapport with the Masters. It is through meditation. If our goal in meditation is union with the Eternal, we are already moving in the right direction. The Masters have made it clear that they do not want people thinking of them in a personal way. K.H. wrote: "The cant about 'Masters' must be silently but firmly put down. Let the devotion and service be to that Supreme Spirit alone of which each one is a part" (LMW1:100).

That "devotion and service" puts us into rapport with the work of the Masters. So in meditation, we may first try to center our consciousness in the heart and become aware of the inner reality that is devoid of malice. Then, trying to get some sense of the Masters' dedication to humanity as a whole, we may enter the sphere of their influence and join them in sending out peace and goodwill to the world. Thinking of the Masters in that way is not a hindrance to their work. It is a way of working with them as colleagues.

If you aspire to become a colleague with the Masters in their work to alleviate the suffering of humanity you can, but if you choose that path, be prepared to meet the challenges that lie ahead. Remember that dauntless courage can overcome every danger, spotless purity can pass through every trial, and strong intellect can solve every difficulty. With an iron, never-failing will, yet being gentle and humble, you may pass through to the other shore if you *try*.

Peace to all beings.

THE MASTERS
AND THE PATH

Transcript of a talk by Dora van Gelder Kunz to the Philadelphia T.S. on May 8, 1955.

I would like to present a few of my own ideas about the Masters and the Path which are somewhat different from what you will find in books. I have been a Theosophist all my life, and the Masters have been real to me as far back as I can remember. I would like to tell you something about my point of view about the Masters and our relationship with them.

The Masters are interested in and their concern is for the whole of humanity. They are not necessarily only interested in us because we are members of the Theosophical Society. Secondly, they are not interested in the past in one way. Their whole dedication is to the future. They are interested in the present, but they are mainly interested in shaping the future. If you read the Mahatma Letters you will notice this idea of shaping the future.

We can be of use to the Masters in a very specific way. The

Masters are beyond the state of personal karma. This is a very important point. They cannot undertake anything which is personal or which would involve them in a personal relationship that they would have to work out. They can only be involved in a personal relationship that is dedicated to the work of humanity. They love you, but if they did something because they only loved you in a personal way, then that would involve them in personal karma and interaction. They are where they are because they are dedicated to humanity.

We as members of the Theosophical Society can be of infinite use to them because the amount that can be accomplished in the physical world depends upon how willing we are to accept karma. If we are pioneers and if we act on the Master's behalf, then we are doing the Master's work, and we are carrying out the karma for that action. Very few people think of it that way. The Masters cannot have personal karma. They cannot be brought back into the vortex of personal relationships. The Theosophical Society is useful, and it will only remain useful if we, the members, are dedicated to that ideal of humanity, and realize that we must be willing to be the agents of karma for the Masters in carrying out their work. Very few of us really realize this relationship. You will find, if you read their letters, that they prefer to think of us as colleagues in a great work.

When you know the Masters, you cannot help but be devoted to them, but they do not want us to worship them, and the Theosophical Society was not meant to be a religious organization. I think that sometimes we put the Masters on a pedestal and feel like little worms below. Some think if they feel a tremendous sense of devotion to the Masters, they can sit in a chair and do nothing, like being in a monastery. That is not enough. The Theosophical Society was not founded on that principle, and it will not fulfill its destiny if we unconsciously treat it like a church. The churches have a tremendous work to fulfill, uplifting the people, giving them that faith and bringing out their devotion. Devotion is a fine thing, but the Masters require a very great deal more. We have to feel a sense of being colleagues with the Masters, engaged in a great work together. As I said before, the more you know about the Masters, you cannot help but have a feeling of love and reverence, but that is not why the Theosophical Society is in existence.

If you have read something about the life of Madame Blavatsky, you know that she referred to her Master as the "Big Boss," and often she didn't like the things she had to do. She was a brilliant person in her way, and she was highly gifted. However, she also had an erratic and tempestuous personality. Some people ask why she was chosen to be the Masters' instrument when she did not live up to the people's idea of what the instrument of the Masters should be. She was the best instrument they could find. She was absolutely devoted to the Master. There was nothing he could not ask of her, in spite of her bad health. She may not have wanted to do it, but there was nothing in the world she would not do if the Master asked her to do it.

The early Theosophical pioneers were devoted, but they were devoted to humanity. The Masters said that the Theosophical Society had to be the bridge between the East and the West. These people were devoted to the cause of bringing the philosophy of the Masters to the people. This is, from my point of view, what the Masters really expect from the Society. They expect us to be a body of people who will do our best, who will do everything possible to bring their philosophy to others, against great odds even, and to be willing to face the karma whether it is right or wrong.

Now, the Masters are real. It is very often difficult for us to make the Masters real because, first of all, very few of us study the literature. How many people have read the Mahatma Letters or the *Letters from the Masters of the Wisdom?* They are basic Theosophy. We talk about wanting to serve the Masters, but we do not bother to find out what the Masters are saying. Few people seem to have read the books. We should go to these original sources. I often advise people to read the Mahatma Letters. The Masters' words are very tough for us to think about. Our preconceived ideas often make a barrier between us, the Path, and the Masters. You start with a certain idea of the Masters, and in meditation you make an image of your preconceived idea of this picture, which is built up out of your background, Christian, Buddhist, etc.

For example, the Masters are holy, but their real holiness may be completely different from what our preconceived idea of holiness is. The real thing is often a shock to us. Be aware of your preconceived ideas. When you meditate upon the Masters, always keep your mind open and see what your impression is instead of making a mental picture of them. Perhaps you will get more of the reality. Nothing worthwhile is easy. Study what the Masters have said, and do not be afraid if you do not understand because it is difficult. Also, you will get a lot of shocks. You know, when we think of somebody holy, we sometimes think of them as rather "namby-pamby." That's what will give you a shock. The Masters say what they think in very, very clear terms. If they think something is wrong, they say it. They called Mr. Hume some strong names. They saw him as he really was. Mr. Hume wanted to be good, but he sometimes closed his eyes to his faults. What did the Masters do? They saw through him, but they worked with him and wrote to him month after month. They never gave up. Did you notice that? Wouldn't we be different? If we see right through someone, we usually say we are through with them. The Masters went straight on with infinite patience, and Mr. Hume finally did something worthwhile. Although he quit the Society, he became one of the leaders in the National Congress in India. That was one part of the work the Masters wanted continued. They wanted India free.

Now, we must not be shocked about it, why shouldn't the Masters be realists? Do you think the Masters are going to take us at our evaluation? They can't, can they? None of us can see ourselves as we really are. When they work with us, and they will work with us, they will comprehend all our weaknesses, they will comprehend all our strengths; and if we will work for the same goal, we shall be able to establish that rapport. It's in the work that the great thing lies.

Now about the Path. The Path is a true thing, and it is open to everybody. But I think it is not virtue which we lack. It is humbleness. Let me explain. One of the dangers is that lots of people become too concerned with whether they have a true experience, whether they are an initiate, a chela, or what. None of that matters. The thing which is true is our relationship and our knowledge, and so many people want those things because they want to be something better. That's a very common human failing. It is a very dangerous one because we are practically never aware of it. If you continually think of it in this personal way, you lose the essence, and eventually you lose the Master. The great thing which comes if you meditate on the Master is an ability to be unafraid to do, to act, to work, and to experience. Think of how you can help. If you get "hide-bound," if you get set or enclosed in rigid ideas, if you get into a permanent state of status quo, then you will slowly close the gateway between yourself and the Masters.

The Masters are working eternally for the future, and they work toward a spiritual change. The important thing for you is not to allow yourself to become "closed." Always live up to what you understand in an experience to be the highest for yourselves, if you want to meet the Master. Be honest with yourself.

Meditation can be of great value, but you cannot say, "I raise my mind to the Buddhi or the Atma" and be there. That is pure nonsense. Just saying the words is not going to get you there. It is the experiencing, the living of it that matters, and when it is real for you, then you really have something. That is the Path.

The Path is for people who are really willing to study. You are not expected to understand every word of these difficult letters from the Masters. But you cannot understand the Masters if you do not make an attempt. Maybe the letter will not make sense the first time you read it. Understanding will come bit by bit if you are really interested in working for the Masters. It is the trying that is important, the trying to lift your mind to the Master's mind. The moment you say, "Oh, this is too difficult," you will defeat yourself. That is the difference between the Theosophical Society in the pioneering days and the members today. In the pioneering days, it was fun for them to have something tough. Do not say that because you do not understand it now that you will not go any further. Don't remain static. We must not remain static because the Masters must work through us and the Theosophical Society.

We should not talk about things we do not understand. Talk bit by bit about things that are in our comprehension. Try to comprehend through your experience, through your personality, through your living. If you once get the feeling of what the Masters are, don't talk about it, but live it. Dedicate yourself from your soul to your physical body to that idea of serving the Masters, trying to do their work through the Theosophical Society. Then, from moment to moment, when the opportunity comes, you will take it. Don't have a lot of preconceived ideas. Keep open. Then whatever is put before you, any kind of work, you will be able to take it in the right way. You will be able to realize that it can be an important experience, and if you are dedicated to understanding something about the Masters, then you will become what I call a Theosophist. There are thousands of members of the Theosophical Society, but there are very few Theosophists. It is very easy to sign a piece of paper and say you want to join the Theosophical Society and that you believe in brotherhood, but brotherhood is something we should live

instead of talking about. The Theosophical Society is the testing ground for brotherhood. It is the place to let ourselves grow,
to let ourselves understand that we are not to be dogmatic, to let
ourselves learn to get along with one another whether we like
one another or not. You must be willing to have differences of
opinion. You must be willing to stand the acid test, even if you
are called names. It is you who are being tested. If you walk out
because one individual says something nasty to you, you are failing the test of brotherhood. Remember, the Theosophical Society is open to everybody. It isn't a closed circle. The people who
stick to the philosophy, who will stick to the Masters through
personalities, these are the people who will get the feeling. They
are the Theosophical "warhorses." That is a compliment. They
are the people who have gone beyond personality. If you could
think of the personalities that you meet as the acid test of your
own character, of your own Theosophy, you would get a different point of view. When something comes up, ask yourself how
you will take it, and ask yourself what it is about you that needs
to be changed. The Masters test us a hundred times on that. If
there were no Theosophical Society, then there would not be
this testing, and perhaps we would have it easier individually, but
we would not have the chance to grow as fast. The lodges of the
Theosophical Society are particularly interesting in the sense of
being a testing ground.

If people are Theosophists in the true sense of the word, they
don't have to talk. They carry something with them. Other people can realize that you as an individual have a philosophy of life.
If you can carry that something which makes you a person who

can be absolutely steady because you have that philosophy of life, and have a tremendous tolerance, and have a devotion to the service of the philosophy of the Masters, then you begin to serve the Masters. Then the lodges you work in will have something of the qualities of the Masters. You then experience the Masters.

How can I try to convey something of the experiencing of the Masters? I shall try to give a brief description of what I think are some of the characteristics of the two Masters that we always talk about, Master K.H. and Master Morya. As I said previously, there has never been a time in my life when the Masters have not been real to me, and I shall try to describe them from my point of view.

Master Morya was the Master of H.P.B. If you read the Mahatma Letters, you get some sense of his personality. As you know, he is an Indian. He is very tall and he comes from a very princely family. I think that if you are in his presence, you have that sense that you are in the presence of somebody who is every inch a king. That feeling really is true because he gives a sense of absolute integrity. That may sound like a strange word to use. What is meant by absolute integrity? All of us have masks. All of us think in terms of little things that are not true. If you are in the Master's presence, for the moment all of that gets wiped out. All of the little things which are not really true, which are not part of what we see as ourselves, are wiped out. If you are in his presence, you meet a person who is so absolutely in the center of his being, who is so absolutely true, that you yourself get the sense of being thrown back into the absolute center of yourself. You get a sense even of the greatness and integrity of yourself. In his presence, you could not think of something childish or mean. Of course, there is also a tremendous sense of strength and of a strength which enables you to carry something through to the end which you have started. It is a strength that has no ending.

In the Master's letters you will notice he is very economical with words. There is also a complete economy in emotion, in movement and in everything. Even in his looks. He has a tremendously noble face, but whatever he feels is not reflected in it. It is a steady face. The facial muscles change very little, because it is the face of a person who is completely at one with himself, and who is cast in a solid granite mold of unity, integrity, and strength.

I think that is a brief personification of the Master Morya.

The Master K.H. is totally different in many respects. Their two personalities could not be more different. Yet, they have a sense of tremendous devotion to one another, as you will notice in the letters. They have been colleagues for so many lives. It is really a beautiful thing to notice how they work together. The Master K.H. is tall, but not as tall as the Master Morya. He has a very noble face. Whatever he feels shows. Pictures could never do him justice because his expression varies from moment to moment. He writes beautiful English in the Mahatma Letters. He has a great feeling for music and the arts. I think that what the Master K.H. conveys is the feeling of love. You might think that if you were in the Master's presence that you would feel very small and shy. Perhaps the Master Morya would give you that feeling a little, but not the Master K.H. You would have a sense of expanding consciousness just as you would with the Master

Morya. But the Master K.H. has the great gift of making a person feel as though you had known him all your life. Don't you think that's a great gift of love? He is a person who is so much a personification of love that it draws from me all the love that I am capable of, and so it draws from any person who comes into contact with him a sense of out-going love. That sense of out-going love is finally a sense of being yourself a perfect being.

We can think about the Masters, and we can meditate about them. In fact, we should think about them. If you are in a quandary, don't necessarily ask them for help, but if you have dedicated your life to the Masters and to the Society and the work (remember that first), then when you are in a quandary think of yourself in the aura of the Master. After all, the Masters have immense auras. If you can develop this feeling of being within the Master's aura, then you could get a sense of what the Master's reaction would be. We would get into touch, but we would not have to ask for help. This is something all of us can try. Think of the Master when you feel very upset about people. If you could put your mind into that state of "in rapport," of that perfect love and harmony, you would get some of the love and harmony within you. Even if the Masters find it necessary to judge people, they see the truth. They are absolute realists. They work with people, and don't judge in the ultimate sense, because they are willing to work with anybody. When you love somebody correctly, you have to be willing to let them be perfectly free. That even applies to the lodge. We have to pull together, but we have to make an atmosphere in which people can grow and in which people are free. If you think there is not enough of that love in your life and in your expression, then think of the Master when you are in a quandary. If you do not know if what you should do is right, then think of the Master Morya, and I think you will get an impression. Often we find it hard to judge what is right because many of us are pulled apart as far as the personality and the soul are concerned. If you have contact with the Master, I think you will get a sense of knowing what is right. We are perfectly right to think of the Masters in that way. Think of them as colleagues. Think of how wonderful it is that we can be engaged in a work with people whom we can learn to understand if we study and if we work. I emphasize work. I think it is only by study and work that we come near the Masters. If we are engaged in their work, then we are in the direct stream of their consciousness. That will automatically become more real from moment to moment. That's why I think we should study, work, have a sense of direction, and a sense of certainty. For Theosophists and the Theosophical Society, the most important thing is, of course, Theosophy, the philosophy, and carrying out the work. If you put that as number one in your life, then I can't see how anything could really throw you off. It is not the individual who is important so much as it is the philosophy and making it a part of your life, part of yourself. Then no human being could throw you off. Slowly, bit by bit, you get that essential certainty, that essential knowledge. That will make all of us something which is so greatly needed today, to be a little like the Masters, to be people of integrity in ourselves, and also to be people who are not afraid to do the things which carry out the Masters' work.

Appendix 2

MEDITATION

If we wish to master meditation, it is wise to begin with simple meditative exercises, a few of which are described in this appendix.

At the beginning, many find that it is easier to meditate in a group than to do it on one's own. Most of us realize that we are affected by the thoughts and feelings of those around us. That is true in a group meditation also. Therefore, if we participate in a group meditation, the experienced members of the group will affect the neophytes by creating an atmosphere conducive to meditation.

Often a meditation group leader will guide the meditation. The suggestions made and the words used may be helpful to some in the group but not to all. In a group meditation, the words and even the suggestions do not matter very much. What is important is to have the group feel united. Therefore it is helpful to begin with a phrase such as, "Let's feel harmony together." It is also important that the group leader use only a few words during the meditation. The leader should describe the meditation first, and then simply say a few words during the meditation to remind the group what to do. If members of the group are not comfortable with the suggestions, then they may simply meditate as best they can while still feeling unity with the group.

As always, a group is greater than the sum of its parts. By meditating together in a group, we can create a powerful center for peace and healing. The first suggested meditation below includes a healing meditation. Often the people we think of in a group meditation are known to us, but that is not always the case. When we do not know one or more of those who are on the healing list, we may wonder how it is possible to reach someone we do not know. Curiously, there is evidence that we can affect those we do not know merely by centering on their names.

Many years ago, a church organist was told that there was a student musician who would be willing to play the organ at Sunday services. The organist wanted an assistant organist, so she happily gave her phone number to the person who said she would pass the number on to the student. Months passed and the student did not contact the organist. Then one evening at dinner with her husband, the organist came out with a non sequitur: "Wonder if that student will ever call about playing the organ?" No sooner did she utter the words than the phone rang. It was the student who thought perhaps she had a wrong number because the husband answered the phone. The student asked, "Is there a Mary there?" Even though the organist and student had never met, the very fact that the student was thinking of "a Mary" connected with Mary, the organist. While this case is rather dramatic, there are countless similar examples of one mind "connecting" with another one in thought. This example and others like it should help to assure us that in meditation we can even reach people we do not know.

Meditating in a group is an excellent place to start, but if we are to become proficient in meditation, we need to learn how to meditate on our own. At first it may seem more difficult than meditating in a group, but if we persist in our efforts, we will soon find that we can do it easily.

Begin by meditating for not more than 5 minutes at a time. As you progress, the time will likely increase automatically to 15 or 20 minutes. The important thing is to do it every day.

Almost everyone has noticed that every place has its own atmosphere. That atmosphere may be created by nature, or it may be created by human thought and feeling. We need only compare the atmosphere in a bar with the atmosphere in a church to realize that this is true. For this reason it is a good idea to select a specific place at home where you will meditate every day. This is recommended because it saturates the place with peaceful energy produced by our meditations. Although this is highly recommended, it is not essential. We can meditate anywhere and at any time, but it is easier to meditate in a spiritual atmosphere than it is on a crowded subway.

It is best to meditate first thing in the morning, or after having morning tea or coffee. One can meditate anytime during the day, but the morning tends to set the tone for the day, and that is why it is recommended to meditate in the morning, even if one meditates again frequently during the day or night.

Here are several forms of meditation that you can do individually or in a group. A full description is given first. A short summary to jog your memory follows the descriptions.

First, be seated in a comfortable position with your back straight. Do not cross your legs. Take a few deep breaths and let go of as much tension as possible. Call to mind a place in nature, or one outside your window, that has given you peace. It may be a beautiful tree or a mountain. Try to be at one with that tree or mountain. Realize its peacefulness, harmony, and lack of anxiety. Try to realize that you, too, are part of nature and of nature's order. Now feel peace going all through you and radiating out from you to your neighborhood.

Before ending, resolve that the peace you have experienced will affect you during the day. If you do that, when you begin to feel upset, the image of the tree will come back to you and for a moment you can let go of the problem and restore a bit of harmony in your psyche. It will not solve the problem, but it may restore the inner harmony that will enable you to solve it.

Do this meditation every day for several weeks or until you feel you can go more deeply. When you think you can do more, try the following: after doing the nature meditation described above, see if you can be centered in the heart, not the physical organ, but near there, as the center of your being. If it helps, imagine that you are a sphere of light with no firm boundaries and feel that you are a center of stillness within that light. Try to identify with the stillness. Say to yourself, "I am that peace itself." The words do not matter; the intention does. Identified with that stillness, nothing can harm you. You are perfectly safe there. In that stillness, you are the nonreactive observer. When thoughts intrude, as they will, simply see them. Do not follow the thoughts. Let them appear as images on a screen that pass by but do not take you with them. If you get caught in a thought and realize it, just let it go without reaction or self-judgment. Go back to the center and be that.

Now you may think of those who need help. Try to think of them at the deepest level you can, rather than at the level of the personality. Do not think of their illness, or even trying to cure their illness. Rather, think of them as whole. Send healing energy to them with the intention that the energy will help them in the way that is best for them. Although we may want the individual to recover physically, that may not be what is right for them. It may be that it is their time to die. Be assured that if you send the healing energy impersonally as compassion, that energy will help them in their transition.

You may end by joining in spirit with people of goodwill all over the world. Be at one with what is good, with what is true, with what is beautiful. Send peace to the world.

Summary:

Take a few deep breaths and relax.

Be at one with nature.

Radiate peace to the world.

(When you have been somewhat successful at this meditation, add the following.)

Center in the heart.

Identify with the peace, *be* the peace itself.

Think of those who need help.

Be at one with all people of goodwill.

Send peace again.

In place of the meditation on nature suggested above, you might try to do a meditation in which you identify with the space of your body. Say, "I *am* that space." (Again, words don't matter. The intent does.)

Now using your creative imagination, feel that you are expanding in all directions until you fill the space of the room. Continue to identify with the space. Expand further outward and become the space of your city, then the earth, then the solar system. Give yourself a few minutes for each step. At each stage, remain identified with the space. Do *not* feel that you are a creature *in* space. You *are* space.

Now reverse the procedure. Come back to the size of the earth, then the city, then the room, then the space of your body.

This space identification meditation tends to center consciousness in the more subtle and enduring part of our human nature, the part that religions call the "immortal soul."

Summary:

Identify with the space of your body.

Expand in all directions and be the space of the building.

Now your city.

Next the earth.

Now the solar system.

Reverse the procedure.

Always identify with the space itself.

Before doing a seed thought meditation, quiet your mind by using the previously suggested meditations or by some other method. Then try to feel centered in the depth of being where there is peace. Next, take a seed thought meditation below (or one of your choosing) and simply ponder it. Rather than analyzing it, try to get an insight into its truth. Give it time. Keep the thought in the back of your mind, perhaps for several days or even more. In moments of quiet, come back to it again and again. If nothing comes of it, drop it for the time being.

Unless otherwise stated, the following quotations are from *The Voice of the Silence*.

Before the soul can hear [we must] become as deaf to roarings as to whispers, to cries of bellowing elephants as to the silvery buzzing of the golden firefly.

When waxing stronger, thy soul glides forth from her secure retreat, and breaking loose from the protecting shrine, extends her silver thread and rushes onward; when beholding her image on the waves of Space she whispers, "This is I," declare, O Disciple, that thy soul is caught in the webs of delusion.

Disciple, close fast thy senses against the great dire heresy of separateness that weans thee from the rest.

Thou canst not travel on the Path before thou hast become that Path itself.

Kill in thyself all memory of past experiences. Look not behind.

Learn above all to separate Head-Learning from Soul-Wisdom, the "Eye" from the "Heart" doctrine.

That which in thee shall live forever, that which in thee knows, for it is knowledge, is not of fleeing life; it is the man that was, that is, and will be, for whom the hour shall never strike.

Be like the ocean which receives all streams and rivers. The ocean's mighty calm remains unmoved; it feels them not.

Restrain by thy Divine thy lower self. Restrain by the Eternal the Divine.

The way to final freedom is within thy SELF. That way begins and ends outside of self.

There is a road, but it is not from here to there. It is from there to here. (Krishnamurti)

And finally, you can use the Zen saying previously mentioned as a seed thought meditation: There is really nothing you must be and there is nothing you must do. There is really nothing you must have and there is nothing you must know. There is really nothing you must become. However, it helps to understand that fire burns, and when it rains, the earth gets wet.

ABBREVIATIONS

Note: All references to the Mahatma Letters come from *Mahatma Letters to A. P. Sinnett from the Mahatmas M. and K.H. in Chronological Sequence*, edited by Vicente Hou Chin.

CW: Helena Petrovna Blavatsky, *Collected Writings*

K.H.: Master Koot Hoomi (*or* Kuthumi)

LMW1: *Letters from the Masters of the Wisdom, 1870–1900.* First series.

LMW2: *Letters from the Masters of the Wisdom.* Second series.

M.: Master Morya

ML: *Mahatma Letters to A. P. Sinnett*

SD: *Secret Doctrine*

SOURCES

Abdill, Edward. *The Secret Gateway: Modern Theosophy and the Ancient Wisdom Tradition*. Wheaton, Ill.: Theosophical Publishing House, Quest Books, 2005.

Algeo, John. Review of *The Masters Revealed* by K. Paul Johnson, in *Theosophical History*, vol. 5, no. 7 (July 1995): 232–247.

____. *Theosophy: An Introductory Study Course*. 4th ed. Wheaton, Ill.: Department of Education, Theosophical Society in America, 2007.

Barborka, Geoffrey A. *The Mahatmas and Their Letters*. Adyar, Chennai: Theosophical Publishing House, 1973.

Besant, Annie. *H. P. Blavatsky and the Masters of the Wisdom*. Adyar, Madras [Chennai]: Theosophical Publishing House, 1918.

Blavatsky, Helena Petrovna. *Collected Writings*. 2nd ed. Vols. 1–14. Wheaton, Ill.: Theosophical Publishing House, 1966, 1977, 1985.

____. *The Key to Theosophy, Being a Clear Exposition, in the Form of Question and Answer, of the Ethics, Science, and Philosophy for the Study of Which the Theosophical Society Has Been Founded*. London: Theosophical Publishing Co., Ltd., 1889. Photographic reproduction, Los Angeles, Calif.: Theosophy Company, 1962.

____. *The Secret Doctrine.* Collected Writings edition, vols. 1–3. Adyar, Chennai: Theosophical Publishing House, 1978–1979.

____. *The Theosophical Glossary.* London, England: 1892. Photographic reproduction, Los Angeles, Calif.: The Theosophy Company, 1971.

____. *The Voice of the Silence.* Introduction and notes by Arya Asanga (A. J. Hamerster). Adyar, Chennai: Theosophical Publishing House, 2005.

Caldwell, Daniel H., comp. *A Casebook of Encounters with the Theosophical Mahatmas.* Blavatsky Study Center, 2003: http://www.blavatskyarchives.com/mastersencounterswith.htm.

____. *The Esoteric World of Madame Blavatsky.* Wheaton, Ill.: Theosophical Publishing House, Quest Books, 2000.

Cleather, Alice Leighton, and Basil Crump. *The Pseudo-Occultism of Alice Bailey.* Manila, Philippines: McCullough Printing Co., 1929.

Codd, Clara. *The Way of the Disciple.* 2nd ed. Adyar, Chennai: Theosophical Publishing House, 2000.

Cranston, Sylvia. *H.P.B.: The Extraordinary Life and Influence of Helena Blavatsky, Founder of the Modern Theosophical Movement.* New York: G. P. Putnam's Sons, 1993.

Farthing, Geoffrey A. *When We Die: Exploring the Great Beyond.* San Diego: Point Loma Publications, 1944.

Fuller, Jean Overton. *Blavatsky and Her Teachers: An Investigative Biography.* London: East-West Publications, in association with Theosophical Publishing House, 1988.

Gomes, Michael. *The Coulomb Case. Theosophical History.* Occasional Papers, vol. 10, 2005.

____. *The Dawning of the Theosophical Movement.* Wheaton, Ill.: Theosophical Publishing House, 1987.

Grimes, John. *A Concise Dictionary of Indian Philosophy: Sanskrit Terms Defined in English.* Rev. ed. Albany: State University of New York Press, 1996.

Harrison, Vernon. *H. P. Blavatsky and the SPR: An Examination of the Hodgson Report of 1885.* Pasadena, Calif.: Theosophical University Press, 1997.

Holy Bible. Reprint of the Authorized King James Version, 1611. Nashville: Thomas Nelson, 1990.

Jinarajadasa, C. *The Story of the Mahatma Letters.* 2nd ed. Adyar, Chennai: Theosophical Publishing House, 2000.

Johnson, K. Paul. *The Masters Revealed: Madame Blavatsky and the Myth of the Great White Lodge.* Albany: State University of New York Press, 1994.

Lachman, Gary. *Madame Blavatsky: The Mother of Modern Spirituality.* New York: Tarcher/Penguin, 2012.

Leadbeater, Charles Webster. *The Masters and the Path.* 3rd ed. Adyar, Chennai: Theosophical Publishing House, 1995.

Letters from the Masters of the Wisdom, 1870–1900. Ed. C. Jinarajadasa. First series. 5th ed. Adyar, Chennai: Theosophical Publishing House, 1964.

Letters from the Masters of the Wisdom. Ed. C. Jinarajadasa. Second series. 2nd ed. Adyar, Chennai: Theosophical Publishing House, 1973.

Mahatma Letters to A. P. Sinnett from the Mahatmas M. and K.H. in Chronological Sequence. Transcribed by A. T. Barker. Ed. Vicente Hao Chin, Jr. Manila, Philippines: Theosophical Publishing House, 1993.

Mills, Joy. *One Hundred Years of Theosophy: A History of the Theosophical Society in America.* Wheaton, Ill.: Theosophical Publishing House, 1987.

———. *Reflections on an Ageless Wisdom: A Commentary on "The Mahatma Letters to A. P. Sinnett."* Wheaton, Ill.: Theosophical Publishing House, Quest Books, 2010.

Nicholson, Shirley J. *Ancient Wisdom: Modern Insight.* Wheaton, Ill.: Theosophical Publishing House, 1985.

Olcott, Henry Steel. *Old Diary Leaves: The History of the Theosophical Society.* 6 vols. Adyar, Chennai: Theosophical Publishing House, 1974–1975.

Smoley, Richard. *Supernatural: Writings on an Unknown History.* New York: Tarcher/Penguin, 2013.

INDEX

ABOUT THE AUTHOR

Edward Abdill, author of *The Secret Gateway: Modern Theosophy and the Ancient Wisdom Tradition*, joined the Theosophical Society in 1959 when he was in his early twenties. He began a regular practice of meditation in 1980, based on a meditation format he learned from Dora Kunz. Abdill was twice president of the New York branch of the Society and has served on the national board of the Theosophical Society in America, as a director from the Northeast and as national vice president. He became an international speaker for the Society in the early 1980s and regularly lectures for the Theosophical Society, both in the United States and abroad. Abdill has written numerous articles for *Quest* magazine, a publication of the Theosophical Society in America, and *The Theosophist*, the international magazine of the Theosophical Society. The Society maintains a video and audio library at www.theosophical.org that contains numerous recordings of his talks and courses. His Foundations of the Ageless Wisdom video course has been used extensively at branches of the Society in this country and internationally. Abdill is a Phi Beta Kappa graduate of New York University. He lives with his wife, Mary, in New York City. His website is www.EdwardAbdill.com.